Who Wants to Diet Anyway?

Alison Woodward

authorHOUSE®

AuthorHouse™ UK Ltd.
500 Avebury Boulevard
Central Milton Keynes, MK9 2BE
www.authorhouse.co.uk
Phone: 08001974150

© 2008 Alison Woodward. All rights reserved.
No part of this book may be reproduced, stored in a retrieval system, or transmitted by any means without the written permission of the author.
First published by AuthorHouse   11/14/2008

Printed in the United States of America
Bloomington, Indiana
This book is printed on acid-free paper.

ISBN: 978-1-4343-9846-8 (sc)

To.

Elizabeth and Owen

Merry Christmas 2008

Love
Alison xx

Table of Contents

Chapter One	4
Chapter Two	11
Chapter Three	25
Chapter Four	36
Chapter Six	61
Chapter Seven	76
Chapter Eight	82
Chapter Nine	93
Chapter Ten	103
Chapter Eleven	112

Chapter One

'OK,' I told myself as I looked at the scales flashing 83.4 kilograms at me. 'You're too fat. Time to go on a diet.' I've said that word again. I don't know how many times I have said that, and every diet ends in disaster. It seems every time I say the D word, my stomach thinks my throat has been cut. I have not even started the diet yet, and I think I'm starving.

'So what diet do I try this time?' I asked myself. I have tried to lose weight before and sometimes I even manage to lose something – usually my will power. But not this time, I promise myself. I'm sure I've said that before as well, but hey, never mind, here goes.

Breakfast. Every diet says you must start the day with a good breakfast (good excuse), right? Then let's see what I can have. Or more to the point, what have we got? I always seem to start a diet when I have not been shopping or when I have just been shopping and have nothing for a diet.

I am going to be really good this time. Two slices of toast with a bit of butter and a spreading of lemon marmalade. Hope this is OK on a diet. Anyway, that's all I have got.

'What's for breakfast, Mum? We are starving.'

'You are,' I think.

I feed the kids, thinking how good their breakfast looks compared to mine.

'OK.' I tell the kids. 'We are going shopping to buy good healthy things to eat to help you children grow big and strong.'

I heard groans from the front room. 'Good healthy things to eat, sounds like Mum is on a diet again,' said one smart kid.

'Wonder how long this one will last,' chirped in another.

'Bet you a fiver we have chips by Saturday,' put in the eldest smart kid.

'No we won't,' I snorted at their lack of encouragement, but I knew deep down they were right. I was useless at dieting. But not this time, I promised myself.

We all piled into the car and set off for the local supermarket. I had a list, and I was going to stick to it and get nothing else.

'Right, fruit and veg first,' I announced.

We went through the different sorts of fruit and veg available with the normal moans of, 'I don't like that and dad won't like that,' but I was not listening. I filled my trolley with all the healthy things I could find in the shop. I agreed to let the kids have their sweets for the week (not a wise thing to do).

I felt very proud of myself for what I had got; the fruit bowl was overflowing and looking good.

My husband came home early and commented on the overflowing fruit bowl, to which the eldest smart kid said, 'Mum is on a diet *again*.'

'Oh!' That was all he said, but his face said it all.

Lunch was a nice little ham salad followed by fruit from the overflowing bowl. I could see by their faces how much they enjoyed their lunch (not) and how much better they felt for swapping their usual hot dog with fried onions and a good-sized chocolate bar for a nice ham salad.

I cleared the table while the kids and husband went in the front room. I decided that some exercise would be good for us on my diet, so we put on our coats and wellies and went for a walk.

We got back about an hour later with our faces a bit pinched. I thought a nice cup of hot chocolate would warm us all up. I put the milk on to boil. Now, do I have a cup? I am a bit cold from the walk, and the salad was not that filling (I'm good with excuses). The hot chocolate was like nectar.

As I finished my hot chocolate with pangs of guilt, the phone rang. 'It's Sharon for you,' my husband told me handing me the phone. 'Hi!' Sharon sang down the phone. Sharon is a little loud and an extrovert but great fun. 'Fancy a bit of shopping after work on

Monday? I need to look for a new dress,' she said. 'Des (Sharon's husband) is taking me out for my birthday.'

'OK,' I replied. 'But I'm on a diet, so no cakes or chips, agreed?'

When the shrieks of laughter had died down, she agreed, saying that McDonald's offered a nice salad, so we could go there.

I thanked her for her support, but thought, how is going to McDonald's going to help?

There would be chips and burgers jumping out at me shouting, 'Eat me, eat me.'

I put the phone down and told the family that I might be a bit late coming home on Monday. My husband said he had Monday off anyway, so I could be out as long as it took Sharon to find a dress. Knowing Sharon that could be a long time.

We spent the rest of the afternoon playing games with the kids, which, by the way, are three girls. The eldest is Kerry, aged fifteen years; the next is Sandra, aged thirteen years; then comes Daisy, aged ten years.

I should tell you a little more about my family; so here goes. My husband's name is Martin. He is forty years old and a little chubby and round in the middle with dark hair that has just a little touch of grey at the sides. He is 6 feet tall. We have been married for seventeen years. My name is Alice. I am thirty-eight years old and 5 foot 4 inches tall with a cuddly appearance (you know what I mean). The girls look more like their dad than they do me. Kerry is slim, and the other two are a bit chubby, but not fat.

'Now what's for dinner?' I asked myself, as it was no good asking that lot. I knew what they would say, and I'd already been bad having hot chocolate.

I opened the door to the cupboard where I kept my cookbooks and rummaged around the back of the shelves. Got it. I knew I had a dieter's cookbook here somewhere. Wiping the three inches of dust from the book, I started to look through it. I had forgotten what a good book it was. Turning the page, I found *Dinner*. I got to work, and in no time, it was ready.

'OK, you lot, dinner is on the table,' I shouted, beaming as I looked at the culinary delight I had made. In they came and sat down.

Placing the dish on the table, I beamed. 'Vegetable lasagne,' I told them. The look on their faces was unbelievable.

'Mummy,' said Daisy, looking up at me, 'I'm going to diet with you, and I ate far too many sweets today, so I think I should miss dinner.' She smiled.

The rest of the family was good. They ate the dinner, and to their own surprise, they enjoyed it, even Daisy.

As I got into bed, I thought about my diet, 'Not too bad a day.' I told myself. 'But no hot chocolate tomorrow, and I must be good when shopping,' I promised myself.

Well, no usual Sunday fry up for me today, but I won't deprive the others I thought when I woke up the next morning. It's not fair. So up I got and started to look for my breakfast before the rest got up.

'I know, I'll have grapefruit,' I said to myself. I cut one in half and looked at it. 'How am I going to eat this with no sugar? But I will. I promised myself.' I was still talking to myself.

I sat down at the table and dug in. I had just put the first spoonful in when the herd came in. 'You enjoying that, love?' Martin asked. I tried to answer, but it was difficult as the fruit was so sharp it was hurting my cheeks. 'Mmm... it's lovely,' I managed to say, trying so hard to stop my face from distorting and my eyes from watering. I finally finished the mouthful with all eyes on me.

'I will get you all your breakfast now,' I said, hoping to escape the fruit. 'No, you finish yours, I can do ours,' Martin said with a giggle. 'I don't mind, really.' I protested, but I lost and had to sit there eating my sour fruit with no sugar with eight beady eyes looking for a hint of a grimace on my face. 'Tomorrow,' I thought, 'I eat alone.'

Normal Sunday morning, washing going round, me slaving over the ironing board, the kids slumped in front of the telly and Martin wandering around the garage pretending to be busy.

After a quick shower, off we went for our Sunday lunchtime drink. I can't wait for my Bacardi and cola. Oh no, the diet. No drink, it is so fattening. 'It will do me good,' I tell myself solemnly. I told Martin that the girls and I would have diet cola. 'It will be a nice change from a regular cola,' I told the girls. 'Not for us. We always have a nice cold cola.' Kerry grinned.

The Sunday joint was just cooked when we got in. The beef, roasted in a little water and no oil, was nice and tender. I peeled the potatoes and prepared the veg and put them on to cook. Next I checked all homework was done and enjoyed a nice cup of tea.

Martin and I served the dinner to more moans from Daisy about having to eat green things. I looked at her and smiled as I said, 'Why do you moan about eating green things? Bogies are green, and you don't have a problem with eating them.'

'Oh, Mum!' shouted the kids.

'Did you have to?' asked Martin.

Lunch over; it was time for a walk. The girls stayed at home, so it was just Martin and me. We chatted as we walked. 'Seriously, love, do you think you will stick to this diet? I mean, it's not that I think you should be on a diet, but you always get upset when it goes wrong.'

I knew what he was trying to say. 'It won't go wrong this time. I promised myself. But thanks for the support.' I kissed him on the cheek and we headed for home.

Back home the girls had washed up and tidied for me. It was a lovely surprise, but I knew there would be a catch.

'Mum, did we do well tidying up for you?' the girls asked. 'Can we have some sweets, please?'

They all chose chocolate. 'Did they plan this while we were out?' I asked myself. 'Of all the sweets they have, they had to choose chocolate? Why not one of those gunky sour things?' I moaned away to myself as I walked around the kitchen. I looked up at the calendar. 'Oh great, my monthly's due. No wonder I'm getting so grumpy. I will need chocolate to survive. Wonder how many low-fat chocolate bars I would be allowed in a day.'

I picked myself up a bit as I got tea ready. 'I am doing so well today,' I praised myself for a change. 'No excuses, no hot chocolate and not even a taste of a roast potato.' I was so pleased with myself; I popped a small chocolate covered cake in my mouth without even thinking about it. 'Oh, why did I do that?' I shrieked when I realised what I had done.

I watched the family munching their way through sandwiches, cakes and biscuits. I never knew how much saliva one person could make. I was sure that it was not my boiled eggs that were making my mouth water so much.

I was woken up by the sound of Martin laughing. I looked at him blankly to see what was going on.

'I'm sorry,' he said. 'But every time someone eats something, you mimic them as if you have not eaten. Are you sure you don't want to swap those eggs for some tea with us?'

'Not at all,' I assured him as I looked at the cake plate. 'It will be worth it in the end.' I hoped.

Tucked in bed, I thought about work and going shopping with Sharon. What a Monday this would be.

Well, shopping was not as bad as I had imagined. Sharon chose a dress in no time. Work was a nightmare. We were told that twenty jobs would be lost this week. I know I have moaned about my job in the clothes shop, but it is a wage at the end of the week, and if not for the job, I wouldn't have met Sharon and had such a good friend. But I would have to see what would happen on Friday.

I started the day well, having my sour grapefruit on my own. Well, not that sour, really. I did sprinkle a little sugar on well, a big sugar, really. I could only find a dessertspoon, you understand. No one was up, so they will never know and I'm not likely to tell them. The girls were abnormally good this morning, and Martin was very helpful. It worries me when they are like this.

I went to work all set for a good day's dieting with my lunch box full of fruit and a healthy sandwich. That will see me to my salad with Sharon. How I live in a dream world, by three o'clock this afternoon I was sure I was going to die of starvation. I have read lots of times that after three days your diet gets easier, who are these people trying to kid?

At last it was five o'clock and time to meet Sharon. 'I'm starving,' I told her. 'Good, me too,' she replied. 'I don't fancy salads,' she said. 'I've had such a day.' She smiled. 'What about a nice drink and scampi and chips before we hit the shops?'

'Oh lord, why me?' I asked. I'm so hungry, and scampi and chips are my favourites. How am I going to say no. 'OK, let's go. Well, it is my dinner, you know.'

We went to a nice little pub, a quiet place that was a bit oldie worldy. 'Do you have a menu, please?' I asked the little plump lady behind the bar. 'Yes, love, at the end of the bar,' she smiled pointing a chubby finger at the menus.

She turned to Sharon and asked, 'Now what would you like?'

'I will have a vodka and orange, and she will have a Bacardi and cola.' She smiled.

'No thank you. I will have a diet cola, please,' I said. Sharon nearly fell to the floor in shock, but I had been thinking that she always did this to me. I mean, she is a good friend, but if I'm trying to lose weight, she always brings me to a pub for lunch. Then I have chips and stuff. But not this time. I will be strong.

Sharon was a little quiet as we ordered our dinner. She had the scampi and I had the seafood salad. I was glad I had chosen it as it was very nice and made a change to having chips. It felt good to say 'no' to my favourite dinner. It was something of a hurdle I had just jumped, and it made me feel good.

Sharon soon perked up as we shopped for her dress. She had to have a size bigger than before. I joked with her about having the scampi and not the salad. She just laughed and told me to shut up.

Sharon chose a simple, knee-length black dress, nothing out of the ordinary, but it looked very nice on her.

'Are you going to treat yourself? She asked.

'Maybe, when I'm thin,' I joked.

I got home at about half past eight that evening feeling very proud of myself. It was something I'd not felt for a long while.

I had a cup of tea with the family and told them all about my day and my dinner. 'Go Mum,' said Kerry. Everyone else agreed I had done the right thing.

'Why didn't you get yourself something today?' Martin asked as we climbed into bed.

'The money doesn't go that far. You know the kind of shops Sharon goes to.'

'I know, love, I'm sorry. If I had more, you could have it.' Martin looked sad.

'I don't need more; I've got you, the kids and my diet. What more could a girl want?' I joked.

Chapter Two

The morning seemed to come so quick. I was sure I had only just gone to sleep.

'Come on, sleepy head,' I shouted to Martin as I got out of the shower.

'OK, I'm up,' he shouted back. 'Yeah, I know what that means.' I laughed. 'You've only just put one foot out of bed.'

'Alice, my love, you know me so well.' Martin giggled as he heaved himself out of bed.

Downstairs, I got breakfast ready. Nothing wonderful. After my good day the day before, I was on a high, so I made scrambled egg on toast.

'Come on, you lot. Breakfast is on the table,' I shouted up the stairs. Then came such a noise, I was sure I had a herd of elephants up there.

'Didn't know I had to diet as well,' Kerry grumped. 'It's not me who's fat, you know.' She looked round the table at us larger ones.

Kerry is, as you know, fifteen, and like most fifteen-year-olds, she thinks she is the boss, the best and knows it all. Kerry is a slim girl with dyed blond hair, and I must say that there are times when I think some of the dye has seeped into her head. (I'm sure you know what I mean.) She does not know the meaning of the word *shy*. She is sarcastic and sometimes unkind.

'I think this is nice for a change,' smiled Daisy.

Daisy is, as you know, the youngest. So unfortunately, she is a bit spoilt. Kerry and Sandra give in to Daisy all the time. She can be a bit of a creep if she thinks it will get the others into trouble or if there is something in it for her. She is a bit chubby, though not too overweight, but the healthy eating will do her good.

Sandra is a placid girl and a great thinker. She is a bit shy, but not unsociable. She never takes anything for granted. She is a bit chubby and will benefit from the healthy eating.

Sandra ate her breakfast with no fuss then got up, 'I'm going to get ready for school now.' She smiled, and then gave me a kiss on the cheek. 'I really enjoyed that. Thanks, Mum.' And off she went.

I got my lunch ready. A ham salad sandwich with no butter, just a spreading of mayonnaise, some fruit and some small pieces of chopped cucumber and carrot in case I get hungry (well, more for when I get hungry).

'See you lot tonight.' I called on my way out.

'You forgot your fruit and veg stall,' Martin shouted after me. 'Oh sorry, I meant your lunch.' He giggled.

'Ha ha, very funny.' I replied, taking the box.

Not a bad day on the whole. I stuck to my lunch and no extras. Is it me or do people who are slim look even thinner when you're on a diet?

I'm sure I've never noticed before how so many people that I work with are so thin. I looked at them with envy, at their nice fitting clothes and their figure hugging jackets. I looked at myself in my baggy clothes. I always wear baggy things to hide my lumps and bumps that are in the wrong places. I thought to myself, not long and I can dump these marques for some real clothes, or maybe I can sell them to a circus. I felt a little down but made myself think of how well I was doing.

We were all told that on Friday, we would be getting letters about the redundancies and who was going and who was staying.

I got home and told Martin about the letters. Things were hard enough with us both working; they would be much harder if I lost my job. I started thinking about who would be the best to go. Sharon should go, I thought. I know she's my friend, but she has no children and Des has a very good job. She only works so she won't get bored.

'Come on, love, don't worry so.' Martin tried to cheer me up, but I was still worried.

I got dinner ready without paying any attention to what I was doing. I was deep in thought.

'Dinner is on the table.' I yelled above the noise of the telly.

'Yes! I won! I won!' Kerry was singing.

'What? What are you on about? What have you won?'

'Don't you remember?' she shrieked. 'Last Saturday, I bet five pounds that we would have chips by this Saturday, and we have.'

'Who did you bet with?' I asked.

'The girls. So pay up, you two. That's two pounds and fifty pence from each of you, please,' she said, holding out her hand.

While all this was going on, I looked at the dinner. How easy it was to just cook what I was used to. The only good thing was that I was not very hungry because I was so worried about work.

Martin and the girls tucked in, and the younger two promised to pay Kerry when they get their pocket money.

I ate very little, just picked, really. Normally I would have eaten a mountain of pie and chips with gravy running down from the top, looking something like Mount Everest with an avalanche, but not tonight.

The next couple of days went by without my really knowing. All of us at work talked about what the letters might say, and why each one of us couldn't afford to lose our jobs.

When I went home in the evenings I cooked and cleaned as usual, still hardly eating anything, but I did make sure I watched what I cooked—good food, no chips.

At last on Friday, I got up and got ready for work. 'What if this is the last time I do this for a while?' I asked Martin.

'Well, you will just have to clean and bake every day.' He grinned.

Martin loves home-cooked food, and there is nothing he likes more than home-baked cakes.

'Yes, that's true. I could catch up on all the jobs that need doing, and I could do baked apples,' I agreed, giggling.

'You know what I was getting at,' he said, hugging me. 'You feel like you've lost weight. Have you weighed yourself?'

'No, not yet, but I've hardly eaten this week, so maybe I have lost something. 'I'm off now. Wish me luck!' I shouted as I headed for the door.

'Good luck!' Martin and the girls called back.

I got to work feeling a little uneasy not knowing when the letters would be brought round. We all had a cup of tea and talked about what we would do if we were sacked. We expressed our worries and talked about job-hunting, but not Sharon; she said she and Des had decided to go on a nice long holiday if she was the unlucky one. Well, she should have kept quiet. I could not possibly repeat some of the comments she got. Besides, I didn't even know what some of them meant.

As we all got up to start work, the door opened and in came the shop floor manager holding a bundle of letters. I could not help but have butterflies. I know it's mad at my age, but I needed this job. It's never been the best job, but it helps keep the boat afloat.

I sat down with my letter and opened it with uneasy hands. As I looked about the silent room, I could see we all felt the same. We were going to lose some good friends. I don't even know what I was thinking as I read my letter.

When I arrived home Martin opened the front door. 'You're early.' He smiled. I just looked at him, and he knew.

'We will be OK; I know you will find a job in no time,' he said, hugging me.

'I have not been out of work for years; I was settled there.' I moaned. 'We didn't even have to work any notice, just go home.'

'Tell you what: I will get the exercise stuff out so you can do an hour or two every day,' he said, trying to cheer me up.

I watched as he left for work, and suddenly I was alone. 'OK, where shall I start?' I thought aloud.

'I will do the bathroom like I keep saying I will.' Off I went armed with all sorts of cleaning things.

'Well, that looks good! I'm glad I did that,' I told myself. But then I was starving and I needed food.

Rummaging around the cupboards, I found some tomato soup, 'That will be good for my diet, not too fattening,' I thought.

'Now I fancy something sweet, like chocolate. I have worked hard and been really good,' I thought aloud. 'OK, I know, I know I only did well out of worry, but I still did well!' I looked around for something; you could tell it was a shopping day tomorrow; there was not much in the house to eat.

What luck! I found some chocolate biscuits at the back of the cupboard. I didn't really want the biscuits, I only wanted the chocolate, and so I had an idea. No, I didn't put them back, although I should have done. Instead, I made a cup of tea and then I scraped all the chocolate off the biscuits with my teeth. Then I licked them to make sure I had not left any chocolate.

They tasted so good and made me feel like a child again. I looked at the now-boring biscuits. I can't waste them, I thought. I'm unemployed now. 'Oh, what the heck,' I thought aloud, and dunked them in my tea and ate them all.

I was just enjoying the peace and quiet when the kids came in.

'Oh hello, Mum. What you doing at home? Are you not well?' asked a very surprised Sandra.

'No, I'm fine. Just unemployed,' I replied.

'Mum!' shouted Kerry from the kitchen. 'I saved five biscuits in the back of the cupboard. Have you seen them?'

'No, love, I haven't. Your dad might have eaten them,' I lied, hoping I wouldn't go red. 'I will get some tomorrow.'

'He always does that. He is such a pig!' she moaned away to herself.

I felt awful blaming him, but I couldn't be found out.

Martin came in just in time for dinner. 'How was your first day of being a lady of leisure?'

'It was quiet, but busy. Your dinner is on the table.' I smiled.

To my surprise, everyone loved the dinner – just a simple dish of pasta with bacon pieces and cheese on top. It was great.

I went to bed feeling guilty about the biscuits. I told Martin about it, and thankfully, he saw the funny side.

Saturday came again, and it was time to weigh in. With a deep breath, I stepped on the scales very gently. I don't know why I stepped gently – it wouldn't have made me any lighter, but anything was worth a try.

'Yes, I've lost 1 kilogram!' I sang around the kitchen.

'See, told you that you felt thinner,' Martin said, putting the kettle on.

I felt very pleased with myself. I knew 1 kilogram was not a lot, but for me, it was an achievement. Well, for me, it was a miracle!

Martin and I had breakfast on our own; we enjoyed boiled eggs and toast.

One by one the kids got up. It seemed like I was doing breakfast forever. One had boiled eggs, one had just toast and the other wanted egg, bacon, toast and beans, but ended up with corn flakes.

'OK, who's coming shopping?' I asked the wall, seeing as the kids were watching telly, I thought I would get a better reply from the wall.

'That's fine. If none of you wants to come, me and your dad will go.' Still no reply.

'You can do your homework and a bit of tidying up for me.' Little response. They looked at me like I had just dyed my hair green.

To my surprise, they agreed to stay and clean the house, so off Martin and I went.

As we entered the shop, the smell of freshly cooked bread hit me. Oh, it smelled so good! I had to get a nice uncut loaf (we all know what that leads to). It was still warm in my hands. How I didn't take a huge bite, I don't know.

'Is it me, love, or don't this fruit and veg look so good this week?'

'Oh please, no more fruit. The bowl is still overflowing,' he replied.

He was right the fruit was still sitting in the bowl from last week. It was not being eaten like I was hoping it would be.

'You're right! I will sort it out when we get in,' I agreed.

I found myself looking in other people's trolleys, thinking to myself, 'No wonder you look like me with all that junk food in your trolley', or 'How can you eat that lot and be so skinny. Bet she's bulimic or shopping for someone else, she's anorexic, really,' I thought aloud. I had to stop myself from looking into the trolleys. I was simply causing myself pain.

I'm sure chocolate and biscuits have legs and jump in your trolley as you pass by; I don't remember putting them in the trolley. Martin must have.

'Do we need all this chocolate and biscuits, love?' Martin asked.

'I thought you put them in. I don't remember putting them in. They must have jumped in on their own,' I said.

'Yes, love, that must be what happened.' He smiled.

'Anyway, I could do some baking with them, and the girls can have a bar each.'

'One bar a day, is it?' He grinned.

We got back to a sparkling home and three beaming kids. 'We did it nice for you.' said Daisy

'Thank you, girls. I do appreciate it; it looks great!' I looked at them. 'What's the catch?'

'No catch, only we are hungry, and we hoped you had got something nice for lunch,' Daisy said looking at me with puppy dog eyes.

'Yes, I have got something nice, a thick vegetable soup.' I smiled to myself as I went into the kitchen. I could just imagine the look on their faces.

'It's good for you, and seeing as I have lost 1 kilogram this week. That's two pounds in my day.'

'Yes, your mother has lost two pounds this week; she just spent it on chocolate! Oh, sorry. Not that sort of two pounds. Silly me, I got it wrong. Martin and the girls were giggling.

We ate our lunch with the usual moaning that if they had to eat many more vegetables, then they would turn into one. Personally, there are days when I thought that they had turned into animals, so vegetables would be a nice change. But at least they are quiet.

'OK, who wants to go to the market this afternoon?' I asked.

'Yeah, please!' Seemed they all wanted to go.

I had some redundancy money that we were going to use to pay up for some things, but now we were going to get the girls some things and use it for a holiday, though nothing posh. I didn't get that much.

We got to the market and found it very crowded.

Why do fried onions always smell horrid when you're not hungry, but doughnuts always smell yummy?

I tried to concentrate on the things the girls were showing me, but the aroma of the doughnuts was distracting me. I had to do something.

'Who can smell those lovely doughnuts?' I asked.

'We can! Are we going to have some? Pleeeeaaase!' came the reply.

'Do you really want some? They are no good for dieting.' I was trying to sound like I was being good, but I was hoping no one could tell what I was up to.

'But we are not dieting, Mum. You are.' Kerry smiled.

I looked at her out the corner of my eye. 'How many should we have?' I asked Martin.

'Six for a pound. That's one each and one to fight over!' He chuckled.

'Only one? But, Daddy, I would really like two,' Daisy said, looking up at him.

'OK, two!' he said.

Yes, I thought, I'm glad Daisy said it. If it had been one of the others, he might not have given in.

My mouth was watering just thinking about biting into one or maybe two of those doughnuts. If I work it right and everyone else is munching, then they might not notice me having two.

I was awakened by the sound of Martin's voice. It was like a long way off, 'Eight doughnuts, please,' he said. No, I must have heard wrong, who didn't want any?

I looked at him just as he turned to me and smiled, 'you didn't want any, did you? Seeing that you have done so well this week.'

'No, no of course not!' I lied. I could have slapped him… him munching on doughnuts.

I watched as he put the doughnut in his mouth and took a bite. The temptation was too much. Martin held his doughnut in his hand as I looked at it. I don't know what happened, and I couldn't have stopped myself even if I had wanted to, but as quick as a flash, I leant over and took one almighty bite out of his doughnut. Boy did that taste good!

'Hey, what do you think you're doing?' He looked shocked.

'Testing your doughnut just to make sure there is nothing wrong with it, you understand. I knew you wouldn't mind because you love me,' I said, fluttering my eyelashes at him.

'Well, it's a good job I do.'

We finally finished at the market and went off to get the holiday brochures and took them home to look at.

It took us ages to agree on a place to go, but we finally agreed on France. I couldn't wait to go and we had only just agreed upon a vacation, let alone having booked it yet.

'Do you know we have not had a holiday in six years?' I said to Martin.

He replied, 'I know, it's only three weeks until the Easter holidays, so not too long to wait.'

Oh no! Just three weeks to lose weight. I was worrying around the kitchen.

Martin helped me get dinner. 'We need something healthy. I must lose weight for the holiday. It might be warm; sometimes it is in early April.'

Dinner was good – boiled potatoes, salad and chicken followed by fresh fruit salad that I made from a few good fruits that were in the overflowing fruit bowl.

We settled down in front of the telly for our usual Saturday-night viewing. I'm sure nearly all the ads were about food. What are these people trying to do to me?

'Dad, do you think they sell nice Easter eggs in France?' Daisy asked.

'More than likely, but don't get too carried away. We haven't even booked it yet,' Martin answered.

Great, first the telly shows food all evening and then the kids start on about chocolate. I think I will just read my book and feel sorry for myself, I thought.

As hard as I tried, I could not stop thinking about the chocolate in the fridge, then about how good I would have to be for the holiday. I was sure this diet was going to send me mad or already had.

I went to bed feeling pleased with myself. I never touched a piece of chocolate all night. The kids had theirs, and I tried not to stare at them as they ate, but it was so hard.

Then it was Sunday again. I lay in till about nine o'clock, and then I wandered into the kitchen, made myself a cup of tea and put the computer on.

'What you doing, Mum?' Kerry was up, smiling. She must have been unwell – teenagers don't do smiling at their mums unless they want something.

'I'm going to book the holiday on the Internet. It might be cheaper; sometimes it is.' I smiled at her.

'Can I look with you? I might be able to help choose a place.' She was still smiling.

Now I was getting worried. Kerry was smiling and wanting to help. It was one of two things: she wanted money, or she had a boyfriend! I would find out by the end of the day.

Kerry and I looked at a lot of places, but in the end we agreed on Normandy. I didn't know about the others, but we liked it. It looked so green and pretty, a nice little cottage in the middle of nowhere but not too far from the beach, and the price was good too.

One by one the others got up and wandered around with cups of coffee and bowls of cereals, still half asleep.

'We are not getting dressed today; we are going to stay in our nightclothes all day,' Sandra announced.

'Oh, OK. Dad and I will go to the beach on our own then.' I smiled.

'To the beach, in this weather?' a surprised Kerry said.

'What do you mean in this weather? It's only a bit of wind; it will blow the cobwebs away,' I said.

'That's not all it will blow away!' Martin had come into the room.

'You're up then. Anyway, don't be boring. The fresh air will do us good.'

'And you're not going to get much fresher than that,' he grumped.

We all bundled into the car and set off for the beach. I did notice on the way that the trees were blowing a little more than they had been at home. Well, actually a lot more, but I said nothing and hoped the others would not notice.

We had a nice stroll along the beach, well, more of a little trot as we were being blown along by the wind.

Martin had remembered the kites; we had great fun with them. We were there for about three hours.

We took a stroll along the seafront in hope that the wind would be less wild there, but we were wrong. Somehow we did manage to stay on our feet, though I don't mind telling you that it took some doing!

I was hungry, but my imagination was running wild. I was sure I could smell chips, but no chip shop would be open on such a windy Sunday in the middle of March. This was the best place to be away from all the temptations in the fridge. I realised how wrong I was when just a way ahead, a chip shop was open and the aroma made my tummy and my kids go mad!

'Can we have fish and chips, please?' Martin looked at me with hope.

We walked back to the car, eating our fish and chips. They were warm and delicious, and I was good, as I only had a small bag of chips.

'Diet going well, Mum?' giggled Daisy.

'I'm not being rude, but you don't seem to be trying very hard with your diet,' added Kerry.

'That was not very kind.' Sandra was angry; that sort of thing always upsets her.

'Don't worry, love, she is right, really.' I smiled at Sandra.

At home I felt a bit down and guilty about what I had eaten over the week. I felt useless at dieting and useless at everything. I went for a bath. I just wanted to be on my own.

I didn't say much for the rest of the day. I got things ready for school and did this and that, then I had an early night.

'Breakfast!' I yelled at about half past seven. I had been up since six o'clock thinking about my so-called diet.

I have decided to try those slimming drink things. I have heard that they work well, so after everyone had gone to their various places I went to the shop.

Back at home with my carrier bag full of tinned powder, I read the instructions and mixed myself a chocolate-flavoured drink with cold milk.

The taste was not too bad, not too good either, but I can't have it all on a diet.

It has been about two hours since I drank my breakfast and I feel like I have not eaten for a week. But I read somewhere once that if you are hungry your body starts to use the fat you have stored. So I will just have to be hungry, at least for another hour or so.

I have done the housework, had at least a pint of water and been to the loo about ten times. I will have legs like sticks if I keep weeing like this, as the loo is upstairs.

Hurray! It's time for lunch, strawberry flavour this time; I'm changing flavours so I don't get bored. The door opened and in came Martin for his lunch.

'What are you drinking?' He was looking in my glass with a turned up nose.

'I decided to try these diet drinks, I got a few tins so they will last a while.' I smiled hoping for encouragement.

'What are they like?' He was still screwing his nose up.

'Not too bad.' I would have preferred a McDonald's shake, but there we go.

'I'm really going to give this a good go.' I was trying to sound positive.

'I bet I will find those tins in the cupboard out of date and not even opened.' He grinned.

I just ignored him and drank my lunch.

Martin went back to work, and I cleared away. I was fed up with cleaning, so I thought I would make the kids some buns.

I got to work getting all the ingredients out and the mixer ready. Now what is one to make? I know, plain buns. Then I will put a chocolate square into each one. That will make a change.

I got the bars of chocolate from the fridge, made the mixture, put it in the bun cases. Then I had to put the chocolate in the bun, but the squares were too big. 'OK, Alice, what are you going to do about this?' I was talking to myself again.

I went in search for my nice sharp knife, but I couldn't find it anywhere in the kitchen. OK, only one thing for it, I picked up a chocolate square and nibbled on one side (it did taste good). Still too big. A bit more nibbling but now it's too small. I decided to just eat that bit because I can't waste. I'm unemployed. By the time I had the size right, half the bar was gone. I finished the cakes. I had to try one to make sure they were OK for the children. They were nice, but a bit sickly after four, or was it all the chocolate, I was trying to get right.

The kids loved the cakes. Aren't you going to try one? Just one won't hurt,' Daisy said.

'No, love, not even one. I'm trying to keep off chocolate.' I lied.

I tried to make up for all the chocolate by having salad for tea, but to make up for that amount I should not have had any tea.

The next few days were very much the same with housework, milkshake, followed by more housework. I was so bored. I had done all the jobs I wanted to do. There was only so much housework you could do in a day; more like only so much you'd want to do in a day.

Thursday came, and I took myself to the job centre. Housework was driving me mad. I looked at all the jobs listed, but nothing was for me. So I left and went window-shopping until I came to the baker's. It was lunchtime and I didn't have a milkshake on me (what a shame – not). I thought, I could have a cheese salad roll. That's not too bad.

The roll was nice but not as nice as the iced ring doughnut I had for pudding. A girl needs a pudding.

I did stop in the fruit shop to get some fruit to make a tart for tea. I thought that would be nice after jacket potatoes and fish in sauce. I wonder who will moan first about tea.

I sat myself down in front of an old movie with a large cup of tea and a box of tissues (bet you, though, I was going to a box of chocolates).

The film was a weepy one and food makes you feel better after a weepy movie. Just one thin slice of fruit bread and a scraping of spread. That should do it.

I was just finishing my second chunk of fruit bread with a good spreading of butter on it when the rabble came in.

'Caught you. I'm telling Dad,' giggled Daisy.

'I don't care,' I joked with her.

The phone rang as we finished dinner. It was my sister. She had found a nice little gym not too far away and it was cheap. Did I want to go with her?

Not really, as she is thin and doesn't need to go. She makes me feel like a hippo, but she wants to go to keep fit and I need to go anyway. It will get me out and away from the housework. She is picking me up on Monday evening.

'You are doing well this week,' Martin told me as we cleared the table.

'Do you think so?' If only he knew, bless him!

'You sure you don't mind me going to the gym on Monday? After all, you will be stuck with the kids,' I said.

'Of course not. Go and enjoy yourself.'

Enjoy myself, is he mad? This is self-punishment for being a pig and eating too much. For a start, I'm going with my skinny sister. How can you enjoy puffing your head off like an old boiler, feeling like you're having a heart attack and then pain for days after in places that you never even knew you had muscles, and he says enjoy.

Chapter Three

Friday was a nice day, so I did no housework. I did the garden instead, which I did enjoy until I tried to stand straight. I was sure I would be stooped forever. My arms ached, my back was killing me and I was shattered. I do need to go to the gym, I'm so unfit. Oh God, the gym will kill me for sure.

I was pleased with myself. I stuck to my milkshakes, but they didn't seem to taste any better as the weeks went on.

I had a nice long soak in the bath and wondered what to feed my family tonight.

When everyone got home, they were glad it was the weekend. As for me, it made no difference; every day was the same.

'OK, you lot. Dinner,' I yelled.

They came bounding to the table like a pack of starving dogs, but the kids had school dinner and Martin had McDonald's for lunch. Maybe I should give them all a milkshake. That will sort them out.

'What have we got for dinner, Mum?' asked Sandra.

'Vegetable curry and rice,' I said, very pleased with my efforts to feed my family.

'Wish I hadn't asked,' I heard Sandra whisper to Kerry. 'I wish you hadn't as well,' she answered.

The curry was very nice and every bit was eaten.

'That was lovely. Can we have it again sometime?' asked Kerry.

You could have knocked me down with a feather. After all the moaning they did, they go and like it.

Kerry was still being nice (well, as nice as Kerry can be) and I still hadn't found out why, it was starting to bug me. I have to know soon.

We spent the rest of the evening playing cards with the girls. Martin opened a bottle of wine for us and the girls had cola. It was really a good evening.

Saturday already. I'm not going to weigh myself today. I think every two weeks will be best for me.

I feel like I have lost weight. My clothes fit better, but I still have a long way to go.

I made my milkshake for breakfast. I'm sure the powder is growing in the tin. I don't seem to be getting near the bottom, and it's like the magic porridge pot.

'Can you all get your own breakfast today? I'm just popping to the shop,' I told whoever was listening.

I got home and started looking in the job paper I had just got. Not a lot in it for a woman with no skills, but I won't get upset about it. I can look better after the holiday. Just two weeks to go.

Lovely day, so I did more gardening. I don't know why I still hurt from yesterday.

'What's for lunch, Mum? It's two o'clock, and we are starving.'

It is two o'clock already, and I was enjoying doing the garden, even though it was a bit chilly. 'OK, I'm just coming.'

I went in and upstairs to wash my hands. I could hear the girls whispering and shushing each other. 'What are they up to now?' I thought to myself as I went down again. I went in the dining room to get to the kitchen. The girls were standing by the table, all smiles. 'Surprise!' they shouted. 'We did lunch for you as you were so busy in the garden,' they chorused.

The table looked lovely with ham salad sandwiches, and they had put crisps in a bowl, small plate of cake and a fruit salad they made themselves.

'Thank you girls. It all looks good. Where's your dad?'

'I'm here. I heard the girls shout they were starving, so I've come to help get the lunch,' he said has he came in.

'Oh, wow! Who did this?' He asked, looking very pleased.

'We did.' They were beaming.

I didn't have the heart to tell them I was on the powdered milk, and anyway the food they had done was not bad, maybe the better eating is paying off.

I had a sandwich, a few crisps and some fruit salad. I'm sure it tasted better because I didn't have to do it.

'Seeing as you girls made such a great lunch, dad and I will clear away.'

'Will we?' Martin looked at me with hope that I was joking.

Martin and I cleared away chatting about our lunch.

'You did well with your lunch. You didn't eat as much as you would normally.' Martin was smiling at me.

'I know. I think the diet is working. I seem to fill up quicker. Don't know how long it will last though,' I giggled.

We finished up in the garden and did some washing. The kids did their homework, so everything was done and tidied away by six.

'OK, you lot, get your coats on,' Martin told the girls.

'Where are we going?' asked Daisy.

'You will see,' we giggled.

We pulled up at the bowling alley, the kids squalled with delight. We played a few games. Sandra won most so we teased her about cheating. She took it all in good fun then we took them to McDonald's.

I was not good in McDonald's. I had large chips, chicken burger, strawberry milkshake (that tasted 100 times better then the ones at home) and a caramel sundae. I felt like a fat pig.

'Glad you fill up quicker now. I hate to think what you would have had if you didn't,' laughed Martin.

We got in about half past ten that night. We were watching telly when I had the most excruciating pain in my chest, and I thought I was going to die.

'It's your own fault. Eating so much. No wonder you have indigestion. You have been so good and now you're not used to all the junk food,' Martin was going on.

'Yes, thank you for your diagnosis. I know all that, Dr Martin, but it's not helping me so just pass the indigestion tables,' I snapped.

I had a terrible night; don't know how many tablets I took.

'I never want McDonald's again,' I told Martin at 3.20 a.m. next morning.

'OK dear, whatever,' he replied knowing full well that if he said, 'Do you want McDonald's?' I would jump at it. He has known me a long time.

Sunday and I'm glad I can stay in bed after such a bad night. Martin was up, so I had the bed all to myself.

I could hear movement and chatting going on, but I took no notice. Then the door flung open and the girls were there with a tray of breakfast and cards and presents. 'Happy Mother's day,' they sang. I had forgotten all about Mother's Day.

'Thank you, sweethearts.' I smiled with bleary, baggy eyes.

'We hadn't.' Martin was behind the girls with a bunch of flowers.

'We tried to keep to your diet; we hope pita bread filled with scrambled egg and grilled bacon is OK,' Daisy explained.

'That's just right, thank you.' I didn't know if it was or not, but it was yummy.

The cards the children had made at school and the gifts Martin had taken them in town to get, when I thought he was just picking them up from school.

I had a photo frame with a photo of the girls in it from Kerry; a new pair of slippers from Sandra (god only knows how I needed them), and Daisy had got me a lovely big box of chocolates.

I thanked them all and said that I would put the chocolates away until I lost more weight.

'Sorry, Mum, I forgot about you dieting. Tell you what, you open them and have one for Mother's Day. Then us girls can have the rest. Oh yeah, Dad can have one.' She smiled.

'That's very kind of you to think of helping me like that, but no thank you. When I open them, you can all have some, deal?'

I sat in my bed giggling to myself over what Daisy had said and eating my breakfast.

Then I remembered some thing that I had forgotten to do. I ran downstairs calling to Martin.

'What on earth's the matter?' He was coming towards me.

'I never got a card or anything for your mum. She will be upset. I just totally forgot.' I was in a panic.

'Don't worry, I've sorted it,' he said. The phone rang, and he answered it.

'Do you want a cup of tea, Mum?' Kerry called from the kitchen.

'Yes, please. I expect your dad will have one as well,' I called back, shocked.

'That was mum on the phone thanking us for the card and flowers we sent.'

There are times I would be lost without him. I'm such a scatterbrain sometimes.

'Did I hear Kerry making tea, again? Is she OK? She has been nice even to me.' He looked worried.

'I know. She has been like this all week. I think she wants money or has a boyfriend. What do you think?' I asked.

'Knowing Kerry, both.'

It turned out Martin was right (I hate it when men are right; they don't let you forget it). Later that day we were talking about the holiday and what to pack when Kerry asked me, 'When we are on holiday, will I be able to have some money to buy my boyfriend a French Easter egg, please?'

'That depends on who he is and if I like him, if we ever meet him.' Martin had put on his firm fatherly voice.

Martin can be a little over protective of the girls, but as he says he was a seventeen-year-old once (I'm amazed he can remember that far back) and he knows how they think.

'You will like him; he is soooo fit.' She was staring into space bleary eyed.

'Anyone would think you're in love looking like that, how old is he?' Martin was not happy.

'We are in love. He is 17 and a bit.' She looked hurt.

'How much is a bit?' He was looking at her.

I sat and waited for the explosion, I know the boy she was on about and I also knew that Martin does not like him. God, I need some chocolate. It was so tense in the room.

'Well, he will be eighteen in June, and I will be sixteen in September, so he's not too old for me,' she said quickly, as she saw the look on her father's face.

We didn't go to the pub again this week. Martin was not in the mood, but I could have murdered a Bacardi or even a couple of brandies, for that matter.

We had lunch with a strained air about us. I was good, no roast potatoes, just lots of veg but the Puddings were not so good. There was chocolate or strawberry whip with shortbread fingers. I had some of everything. I needed the sugar to keep me calm (not a bad excuse).

I cleared the table on my own and was glad of it, as Martin's mood was beginning to get me down.

I was just putting my finger in the bowl that I had made the strawberry whip in, when Sandra came in the kitchen.

'Mum, you're not allowed to do that.' he stopped at the door and was wagging her finger at me.

'Can I have some? Where's the chocolate one? Mum, you haven't, have you?' She was smiling.

I had been caught so I had to confess. I had already cleaned that bowl out with my finger.

I was getting fed up with Martin and his mood, so I told him it was time we took a walk.

We talked about the girls growing up and how he has to accept it. He was better when we got back. He was still worried about her having a boyfriend of that age. Men I ask you!

'I'm off for a long Mother's Day soak in the bath. Call me in an hour so I can sort out tea,' I told whoever was interested.

As I got into the hallway Kerry called me. She put her arms around me and squeezed tight, kissed my cheek and said 'Thanks, Mum. You're the best.' That was the best gift of the day.

With all the hassle of the day, I need to open my chocolates. I took the box from the drawer and opened it carefully so no one would hear me. I smelled the chocolate before I popped one in my mouth. It was like heaven. All the stress just melted away like the smooth chocolate in my mouth. I placed the box on a stool by the bath, and turned the taps on, then popped another sweet in for good measure.

Before I knew it, I had eaten the entire top layer and didn't want any tea. I was feeling a bit sick.

It must have been ten minutes later; Martin was banging on the door.

'Your hour is up, have you gone like a prune yet? Your Mother's Day tea is ready.' He sounded in a much better mood.

'OK, just coming,' I answered. How on earth am I going to have tea? I was still feeling sick from all the chocolates. I could make myself sick, I thought; no, that would be a waste of chocolates. That would be criminal.

I got downstairs to find a lovely tea laid out for me. 'You shouldn't have,' I said.

Everything I loved was there, even a lovely Mother's Day cake in the middle. It looked a lot like Christmas.

I did my best to show how pleased I was with all their hard work, but it was an effort, and I was sure I would be sick at any time. I was thinking that I wish we had a dog then I could have passed things under the table to it and no one would know.

Next morning I woke up still full from all the food I had eaten yesterday. I heaved myself out of bed and into the kitchen. I got breakfast for the kids. There was no way I could face eating at the moment.

Lunchtime and I still was not hungry, so I just kept on with my chores. By the time I had finished the garage, the kids were home.

'You home already? I have not sorted out what to have for dinner yet. Are you starving?' Silly question to ask kids really.

I got them some goodies from yesterday's tea. As I was getting it together, I started to feel shaky. I know what this is, I thought, my friend has this if she doesn't eat for long periods. The doctor said her blood sugar level drops, and so she should have something sweet at once to feel better. That's what I needed then.

I looked in on the kids to make sure they were watching telly or something. Then I stuffed a huge bit of chocolate cake in my mouth. It looked like I had two eggs in there.

'Can I have a drink of cola, please, Mum?' Daisy was on her way into the kitchen. I panicked, opened the fridge door and pretended to be looking for something. I was chewing as fast as I could but swallow no chance.

'Mum, can I have a drink?' she called again. I peered over the fridge at her and nodded, speaking was not an option. 'You OK?' She looked at me. I just nodded again. She went out with a look that said Mum has gone mad.

I stayed in the fridge until I had finished my cake, but I needed something to wash it down. I could not risk being seen trying to get a drink of water. If someone come in then the game would be up. I looked in the fridge, took a long swig from the open wine bottle that did the trick.

I closed the fridge door to find Martin standing there.

'A secret drinker now, are we, or was it to wash the cake down?' He grinned in a knowing way.

'I needed the energy for the gym, and anyway I have not eaten all day,' I told him matter of factly.

'What time you going?'

'My sister Pat is coming for me at seven o'clock this evening. I will have dinner when I get back, if I can still move by then.' I rolled my eyes at him.

Pat was on time. That's unusual for her. I'm sure she will be late for her own funeral. Off we went in our gym clothes; well, Pat was. I was in a baggy T-shirt and jogging bottoms.

'How was it, love?' Martin asked as I came in two hours later.

'Other than being the only one that was a couple of kilograms overweight, it was fine,' I said a bit sarcastically.

'No, I did enjoy it. I must have sweat buckets. There was at one point, however, that I felt an oxygen tank would have helped, but I survived. Did you save me any dinner?'

'Oh, I thought that you would be too tired to eat.'

'Me, too tired to eat? Since when? What you mean is it was so nice that you and the kids scoff the lot?' I smiled at him.

'I can do you beans on toast while you're in the shower, if you want.' He was creeping.

'That would be nice. I would have liked the tuna and pasta bake more, but there we are.' I patted his tummy as I went past.

I felt good when I went to bed, very tired. I slept like a log.

Tuesday morning came quickly. I had pain in every part of me that I could think of. I tried to walk as normal as possible, but my knees refused to bend and my muscles refused to hold me up. I tried to hold onto the banisters, but my arms and shoulders were in sympathy with my legs.

I finally made it into the kitchen. Putting the kettle on was like trying to pick up the table. It was shaking all over the place. 'That's it, they will have to get their own things this morning,' I told the kettle and went to sit down. Even that was an effort. The cheeks of my bum hurt.

I don't know how I got through the week, getting things ready for the holiday. The pain did start to ease off by about Thursday, but it was not altogether gone.

I was good on my diet this week. I don't know if I was trying harder, or whether it was the fact that putting my arms up to my mouth caused so much pain. Whatever the reason, I didn't bother. Either way it worked.

'Do you think they have diet stuff in France?' I asked no one in particular.

'Oh Mum, no one diets on holiday,' Sandra sighed.

She was right. I didn't know anyone who has ever been on a diet on a holiday. What was I thinking? Still, mustn't go mad.

Saturday morning and time to weigh in.

I jumped around the kitchen. In two weeks I had lost 3 kilograms. I was so happy that I was thinking what to have for dinner to celebrate.

I'm still going to be good on my diet today. I won't go mad. I will have a vanilla shake this morning and a chocolate one for lunch.

Noise began to fill the house as the tribe emerged from their rooms, banging and crashing around the kitchen in search for food. They were like a pack of starving wolves.

I sat at the table with my milkshake, willing it to taste like a McDonald's shake, watching them traipse by with cups and bowls or plates with god knows what on them. It was like you see on telly, one person is sitting on his/her own and the rest of the world is whizzing past them.

Finally I got up and started the housework. The front room was like a bomb had hit it, but I was not going to let it annoy me. I was on a high after going on the scales and I was feeling good about myself.

The kids were doing whatever as I cleaned the house, singing away to myself as I finished the bathroom.

'Do you want some tablets for that pain?' came Martin's voice.

'That's very funny. I thought you liked it when I sing. Then you know I'm happy.' I grinned.

'Oh, you were singing. I thought you had hurt yourself.' He laughed at his own wit.

I chased Martin around with my wet cloth that I had cleaned the bathroom with, and I got him good.

'What are you two doing?' asked Sandra.

'I'm just helping your dad to wash. He was horrid about my singing,' I said as I scrubbed Martin's head.

'Is that what the noise was? I thought someone had the cat's tail.' She was laughing.

Well, that's two people who will need a good shower tonight. They smell like lemon bathroom cleaner.

I was surprised how much energy I had, and I felt so much better for it.

We had lunch late. I had milkshake and the others had toasted cheese sandwiches. They did look and smell good, but I stayed focused.

We went to town for the last of the things we needed for the holiday. We agreed that we would try everything French and not take anything English with us.

It was five o'clock, and my tummy was going mad, and to make things worse we still had to go shopping.

We looked at the fruit and veg. I only got a little as we were going away in five days time. We got to the cooked-chicken counter. There was a lady giving away free samples of the new barbecue flavoured chicken. The smell was too much for a starving woman.

'Shall we try the chicken?' asked Martin.

'I will. It is spit roasted, so no oil. Only the flavouring that they put on it.' I smiled sweetly.

It was yummy. I could have eaten more, but you were only allowed one sample each, spoilsport.

'I forgot the sugar. You go to the checkout, I won't be long.' And off I trotted.

I went the long way round to get the sugar and just happened to have to go past the cooked chicken counter again.

'Would you like to try our new flavoured chicken, madam?' the lady asked.

'Yes please, it smells good,' I told her nicely. I had a good-sized piece this time. 'Thank you,' I said as I headed for the sugar.

I had to get back to the family. So that meant that I had to go past the cooked-chicken counter again (what a shame). There were a lot of people at the chicken tasting counter, and to my delight a different lady handing the chicken out. She looked at me and smiled, 'Would you like to try our new flavoured chicken, madam?'

'Oh yes, please. It looks lovely.' I ate it as fast as I could and got back to the others.

'You have been ages,' Kerry moaned.

'Sorry, I couldn't find it. They have moved it,' I lied.

We were next in line at the checkout when the smell of the chicken hit me again.

'Did you get a bottle of wine for tonight?' I was desperate for that chicken.

'No, you can get one if you want; I don't mind,' Martin replied.

'You start putting the shopping up, and I will run and get one.' I was off.

The chicken counter was too far away from the wine section, so I just went to get the wine feeling a bit deflated.

'Good evening, madam. Would you like to take this bag of our new flavoured chicken home to try? We are giving it away as the chicken counter is now closed,' a voice behind me asked.

'Thank you very much. I could smell something good, but I didn't get as far as the chicken counter.' I smiled as sweetly as possible.

I got back just as Martin was finishing putting the shopping on the belt.

'What have you got there?' he asked.

'The chicken we tried earlier. The young lad gave it to me when I was getting the wine.' Now I was not lying.

'Are you sure you didn't go back for another try?' Martin looked at me suspiciously.

'No, I didn't. Look there he is with the chicken,' I grunted as Kerry went to see if she could have some as she knew him from school, bonus.

Martin looked at the lad talking to Kerry and giving her the biggest bag he had. 'Sorry, love.'

'I don't know how you can think that of me, after I have done so well. What do you think I am?' I was trying to sound hurt. It is not easy when you're trying not to laugh and give the game away.

We had the chicken with salad and new potatoes. It was good. We had loads, thanks to Kerry.

I still have not told them about all the chicken. I tried, but then they don't really need to know.

We had the wine. Kids had Cola, and we all played games and had a great evening.

Chapter Four

Sunday again, and a wet one at that. The kids were fed up waiting for the holidays to start.

'We need a laugh on this wet day,' I said shaking an exercise video at them.

'Oh yes, I've just got to see you try to do this,' Kerry was putting the video in the machine.

'Cheeky mare.' I giggled.

Soon we were in stitches trying to do the exercises and trying to keep up. I don't know who got bumped into most. All I know is we are going to have some bruises tomorrow. We were worn out just laughing. I don't think we even managed to do any of the exercises.

We had roast beef for lunch. A mountain of veg (got to keep everyone regular), and this time everyone had boiled potatoes, not just me. Then we had banana custard. That was tasty.

The rain stopped about three o'clock in the afternoon. So we put on our wellies and went for some fresh air. It was refreshing walking after the rain. I started the day thinking it was dull and boring. Then I found the video that was great fun, and now we are strolling along together sharing the day.

I looked at the girls all chatting and laughing and wondered how quickly they are growing up. How much longer will they want to stroll along with us, but that's life, and they have to grow up.

We got back to find a note on the door from Sharon and Des letting us know they were back, as if we cared. Today we were enjoying being a family.

Martin prepared our Sunday tea. He came in with a tray for Kerry, one for Sandra and one for Daisy. Each was piled up with sandwiches, crisps, cakes and goodness knows what else.

'Thanks, Dad.' The girls were delighted, and I would have been with that lot, too.

I couldn't wait to see what delights he had for me. Here he comes with the tray. I was grinning from ear to ear with anticipation.

'Here we are, my love. Two boiled eggs and two crisp breads, just right for your diet.' He looked at me so pleased at his efforts to help.

'Thank you, love. You got it just right.' I was trying to hide the disappointment. I can't even begin to describe the disappointment I felt, but ultimately, he had done the right thing.

Then came the usual Monday morning and an effort to get it all together. The kids didn't want to go to school; Martin didn't want to go to work. Getting different breakfasts for this one and that one. At last, they had all gone out the door. I was feeling frazzled already, and my day had only just begun.

I had just got myself a milkshake for breakfast and was willing it to taste extra good this morning when the doorbell rang. I put my hands on the table, and heaved myself up and slowly dragged myself to the door.

At my doorstep stood a bronzed and very slim Sharon. I could feel my eyes turning green as I thought about how hard I was sort of trying. Shall I slam the door on her or not? Not a chance. She was in before I knew what was happening.

'I'm back.' She breezed into the dining room. She looked at my breakfast with disgust. 'I see you're still struggling with your diet, poor you,' she said with a hint of laughter in her voice.

'Did you have a nice time?' I felt I had to ask, as I put my glass in the kitchen and tried not to pop her on the nose.

'It was great. Too hot. I could hardly eat a thing with the heat. So Des and I sunbathed all day, but that got boring, so I left Des to sunbathe, and I went in search of something else to do. I found someone by the name of John. That's not his real name, I couldn't pronounce his real name...' She was waiting for me to reply, she had a long wait so she continued.

'He owns a gym, and his workout was marvellous. I'm sure you know what I mean.' She was giggling like a schoolgirl and really beginning to annoy me. Her husband loves her with all his heart. He had worked long and hard for her to have everything. I know it has paid off for him as well over the years, but still I was disgusted with her.

'So that's how I lost so much weight,' she went on and on. I felt I had to make coffee just to stop me from strangling her.

'Sharon, I'm glad you had a good holiday, but I'm very busy. Maybe you could go back and get that nice, respectable Sharon back. I think you must have left her there,' I was trying to stay calm.

'Well, sometimes it's good to change, as Elisabeth said. That's a new friend of mine. She and her husband were in the room next door. They have a big boat and a house in France and Spain. She was the one who put me on to John. She knows his friend very well...' She was going on again.

'Sharon, will you please go home. I am trying to pack to go on holiday, and I don't want to know about John or anybody else.' I pushed her out the door and slammed it shut.

I was still fed up with Sharon having lost all that weight and about her behaviour when Martin and the kids came home.

I told Martin about Sharon and why I was fed up. We chattered about it as I got the dinner on the go. We had shepherd's pie, then yoghurt. I just picked at my dinner.

We talked about the holiday, I can't wait for Friday. I need to get away.

By bedtime I was my old self again. I told Martin I was sorry for being silly and green eyed about Sharon. He gave me a kiss and said he loved me the way I was.

Tuesday already. Where did Monday go? I was asking myself.

'Come on, you lot or you will late,' I called up the stairs.

'Morning, Mum. How are you today?' Smiled Sandra.

'I'm fine. Thank you, sweetheart.'

'Not long to our holiday,' Daisy was singing.

Everyone gone and time for me to eat. I was starving so I went in search of food. I found just the thing, Weetabix with a little sugar. They were great.

I was cleaning and singing when the phone broke into the tuneless chorus of my song, Show Me Heaven.

'I don't think I will be home for lunch today, Martin said.

'OK, no worries,' I sang to him.

I finished the upstairs of the house in time for lunch. 'No Martin here for lunch, no Martin to watch what I'm eating.' I was talking to myself again. I must stop this habit, it is starting to worry me..

I cooked two sausages, two rashers of bacon; the toast was in the toaster and just the eggs to do. It has been a long time since I had a fry up.

The sausages were nicely browned, the bacon just a bit crisp, the eggs sunny side up and the toast just a bit burned like I have it. I put a good-sized knob of butter on the toast, and then dipped it in the egg. The egg was dripping onto the plate as I took a long-awaited bite.

'I made it home for lunch.' Martin had come in the door and was staring in total disbelieve.

I looked up at him as the egg dripped off my chin. I couldn't say a thing. I had been well and truly caught in the act.

'So this is what you eat when I'm not here,' he smiled.

I tried to look guilty and sorry, but the look wouldn't come.

'Am I allowed the same,' he asked.

'Yes, I will get it for you.' I rushed off to start his lunch.

We ate our lunch together, just the two of us chatting and laughing. Martin didn't have to go back to work so we spent the rest of the day together. We had a lovely afternoon.

The kids came in from school, all still in good mood, but with only three days to go, I can't blame them.

'Guess what!' Daisy shouted.

'What?' Martin shouted back, and then laughed.

'There is no school on Thursday,' she beamed.

'What do you mean no school?' Martin and I said together.

'The teachers are on strike. Something to do with wanting more pay,' Kerry explained.

'Well, you will all have to help me to get thing ready. The house must be nice, and the packing has to be finished, OK?' I said.

'We could start our holiday on Thursday.' Martin was grinning.

'What do you mean?' asked Sandra.

'Well, it's a long way to the ferry from here, so we could start on our way about 2 o'clock and stay in bed and breakfast for the night. What do you think, girls?'

'I don't know,' I said. 'That means we will have to eat out. That's more out of our holiday money.'

'Oh please, Mum,'' the kids were begging me.

'We will be OK, love,' Martin was begging me as well.

'Oh, OK then.' I had no choice but to give in.

Martin helped me in the kitchen. We were doing sweet and sour pork, and we chatted as we worked.

'I'm worried about the money for the holiday,' I told him.

'I told you; we will be OK for money. Don't go on about it,' he was sharp and cross at me. This was not like him, he was normally understanding.

'Dinner,' I shouted over the chattering of the kids.

'What is this?' asked Sandra screwing her nose up.

'Sweet and sour pork, why?' I asked.

'Hope it's not like the one we have at school. That's disgusting,' she moaned.

'If it is, then your dad made it. If it's nice, then I made it.' I looked at Martin and grinned.

We all ate our dinner. I was good, and mind you I had had a filling lunch.

Martin was OK all evening, still in a bit of a funny mood when we went to bed; so I just let him alone.

I lay in my bed with the alarm ringing, thinking do I have to get up when the bathroom door opened, and in came Martin from the shower. I didn't even realize he was up.

'Come on, sleepy head,' he grinned.

At least he was back to his normal self (if normal is the right word to use). That was something to be grateful for.

'All right, I'm getting up. You make the tea, and I will be there in a minute,' I told him lazily.

I dragged myself downstairs, and started on the kid's breakfast. Just toast today. I don't feel like doing anything else.

'Come and get it,' I yelled.

'Is that it?' asked Kerry.

'Yes, that's it. Unless you want to do something for yourself,' I grunted.

'No, no toast is fine. Thanks, Mum.' She had thought better of starting on me today.

It seemed like a lifetime before they all went out the door. Now it was my turn to eat.

I looked at the milkshake that I had pushed to the back of the cupboard. I didn't really want one but had to do something. My eating was getting bad again. I should never have weighed myself. It has all gone to pot since then.

I drank the milkshake as quickly as possible. Then had a large glass of water to wash the taste away.

I went to town to look about, just to get out of the house really.

'Alice,' a voice was called. I looked round and saw Abbey – a girl I used to work with – waving to me.

'Hi, Abbey.' I waited for her.

'Are you busy? Do you want a coffee?' she asked.

'That would be great.' We went to the coffee shop in the high street; it was a popular place with nice, soft armchairs instead of hard chairs.

We were there for a good couple of hours. Then my tummy started making so much noise it was embarrassing.

'Is that you?' Abbey giggled.

'Yeah, sorry. I'm trying to diet, but I'm so hungry. I've been trying those milkshake things,' I explained.

'Me too. I'm sure they work if you have the willpower, but as I don't have any they don't work.' She giggled.

It was good to talk to somebody who knew what you were on about.

We finally left the coffee shop and wandered about. It was about one o'clock, and the pub at the bottom of the high street had an offer. Scampi and chips or cod and chips or lasagne and salad. Buy one and get the other at half price. Abbey and I looked at each other, linked arms, giggled and strolled into the pub.

We came out full and happy. The food was great. We overdid it a bit on the drink. Abbey had four Malibu and Colas, and I had four Bacardi and colas. We giggled like naughty schoolgirls eating what we were not supposed to. I got home about ten minutes before the kids.

I was just drinking a cup of tea and thinking about how long I had known Abbey but not known what good fun she was when the kids came in like a herd of elephants.

'Hi Mum, where you been? You smell like a pub,' Sandra remarked as she kissed my cheek.

'That's because I have been to a pub.' I smiled.

'Did you have a nice time, or did you stick to your diet?' smirked Kerry.

'Cheeky mare! I had a great time, thank you, and the scampi and chips were lovely.'

Kerry was laughing and shaking her head at me as I got them a drink and some biscuits.

'Dad, Mum has been to the pub today,' Daisy reported to Martin as he came in.

'Oh, has she? Did she have a nice time? And who did she go with?' He was looking at Daisy and winked at me waiting for her to tell him.

'I had a great time. I went with Abbey; I used to work with her. We went for a spot of lunch. It was a nice change.' I smiled.

'Good, what did you have?'

'I was very good. I had seafood.' I tried to look like a good girl.

'That was good. What kind of seafood? It wouldn't have been scampi, by any chance.' He grinned.

'Well, scampi is seafood. It's just the outside bit that's the problem.' Martin just looked at me, and shook his head and grinned to himself.

After all the homework was done, I set about doing the dinner. I was kind to them.

'Seeing as I had chips today, I thought you could as well.' I smiled as I gave them their dinner. They all enjoyed it.

I went to bed and thought that I was not that bad today. A milkshake for breakfast, scampi and chips, four drinks for lunch and no dinner, not that bad, but I could and should do better.

Thursday and a nice lay in as the kids don't have school today. Oh no, I must get up. We are going away today, and I bet the kids won't do much to help, and with Martin at work this morning I have a lot to do.

I got up to the smell of coffee and toast. I went into the kitchen and found Martin piling toast onto a plate.

'What you doing? You're late for work.' I was worried.

'Surprise! I have got the day off, as well.' He kissed my cheek.

He laid the table with butter and jams and whatever else he could find to go on toast. Then he handed me an envelope and said, 'See, I told you we will be alright,' and went off to get the girls up.

I carefully opened the envelope like something nasty would jump out of it, instead I found 500 euros. I sat there staring at it until he came in again.

'Where did you get it from?' I asked.

'I have been saving to make sure we had enough. I know how you worry, you old worry box.' He smiled.

'Now have some breakfast before we get it all together for the off,' he said as he handed me a cup of tea.

'We are going on holiday today,' Sandra was singing as she came in the room.

'No milkshake today, Mum? Started your holiday already?' Kerry giggled.

'Not today. Your dad had this entire breakfast ready when I got up. Can't let it go to waste.' I smiled.

'Yeah, whatever.' Came the reply.

We were all so excited about the holiday, and before we knew it we were all ready to go and it was only one o'clock.

'Whose ready for the off?' called Martin.

'Are we not having any lunch? Asked Sandra.

'Yes, on the way.' Martin smiled.

I looked at him, 'Yes, we can afford it.' He said reading my mind.

Well, it must have taken us all of 3 minutes to be in the car. I don't ever remember seeing my family move so fast.

We had been going for about 10 minutes, and the girls wanted to know where we were going to eat. 'Wait and see,' was all Martin would say. I would have liked to know as well.

About half an hour later we pulled into the car park of a lovely little pub. 'Here we are,' he beamed.

'Oh wow! This looks nice.' The kids liked it.

'How did you know about this little, out-of-the-way place then? Been here before, have we? A nice little pub in the middle of nowhere.' I winked and nudged him jokingly.

'No, come on you daft head. I'm starving.' He laughed and gave me a big kiss.

'Hope you two are not going to be like this on holiday, it's so embarrassing,' moaned Kerry.

The pub was as lovely and pretty inside as it was out. At last I felt my holiday had begun. We sat at a table by the window, and Martin handed the menus out. 'You can have whatever you want,' he told the girls.

'Really, can we have starters and everything?' Daisy didn't know where to begin. There was a lot to choose from, and she liked a lot of what there was.

'We are going to have the best holiday yet.' He smiled.

'Mum, you will have to starve. There's not much on the menu for a diet,' Daisy said matter of factly.

'Thanks, Daisy. Anyway, I'm on my holidays now.' I put my nose in the air pretending to be hurt.

'We thought your holiday started yesterday with your trip to the pub,' teased Kerry.

'Very funny. I'm so hurt now that I'm going to have to have a large Bacardi and cola followed by steak, kidney pie and chips,' I told them.

'That's the Alice I know,' said Martin patting my knee.

The food was great. We never left a scrap. We were a bit sad to go as we were so full up. We could hardly move. So we walked around the car park for 10 minutes to feel better.

About 2 hours later we arrived at the ferry port. It was almost five o'clock. Martin went straight to the ferry terminal.

'What are you doing? Our ferry isn't till ten o'clock tomorrow morning. We are more than a bit early,' I was panicking.

'Don't worry. I know what I'm doing. When you agreed to leave today and not tomorrow I changed the ferry for six this evening. So we will wake up in a French bed and breakfast.' He was pleased with himself.

'Dad, you're the best!' The kids were all trying to hug him, as he drove, not a good thing to do.

The crossing was good (thankfully). The girls were chattering about the holiday. We were having a good start to the holiday, and I was already feeling more relaxed than I had for ages. It was about nine o'clock that night when we booked the bed and breakfast. We were getting a bit hungry.

'McDonald's,' shouted Daisy.

Right opposite the bed and breakfast was a McDonald's. We left our car in the B&B car park and walked over to McDonald's.

Thank heavens it was all the same as in England, so we had little trouble ordering. It was nice and hot. That's something you don't often get.

The kids had burgers, chips and milkshake. Martin went for a burger, potato wedges and Cola. I had… can you guess? I had a lovely chicken salad! There that surprised you didn't it?

We were lucky to get a family room that slept six. It was a nice room. Not very big but pleasantly done up. The kids were asleep in no time. Martin was dozing and I fancied something sweet. 'I know,' I thought to myself, 'I have a big bag of chocolates (just for emergencies, you understand) in my handbag.' These are ones with the crispy shells, so they don't melt everywhere. I opened my bag as quietly as I could and pulled the sweets out. I managed to open them with very little noise. I bit all the shell of one sweet then let the chocolate melt slowly in my mouth. The taste was divine. I put a handful in my mouth at once and chewed a little bit to break the shells. Then I let the chocolate melt again.

'Are you going to share them, or stuff them all to yourself?' Martin was up on his elbows watching me.

'How long you been watching me?' I mumbled with a mouthful of sweets.

'Long enough to see you stuff a handful in, in one go. Now hand some over, or I will wake the kids and tell them.' He laughed.

'Oh, that's blackmail,' I said as I passed him some sweets. Sharing my bag of sweets with one other person was bad enough but with three more... no way! We ate the lot, then had a large drink of water and went to sleep.

Good Friday and we woke up in a French B&B just like Martin said we would. It was a nice day, not very sunny but still warm.

'I wonder if the shops will be open to get the shopping as it's Good Friday,' I was chatting to Martin at breakfast.

'We don't have Good Friday in France,' the waitress told us in perfect English.

'Oh, right. Thank you. Your English is very good,' I told her.

'I have to speak good English as we are close to the ferry port. Lots of French people speak English. We learn it at school.' She smiled.

We chatted for a while then she pointed us in the right direction. The place we were heading for was about 210 miles from the port, so we needed to know where to start.

We completed the journey in about 3 hours. We got a bit lost and only once. We found a big supermarket with a restaurant so we thought we would give it a try.

'This looks good. It's only six euro and fifty cents a head,' Martin was scanning the menu.

'I will order. I have been doing French at school,' Sandra announced pushing her way to the front.

'OK,' I said smiling. I've never seen her so bossy.

Sandra ordered like she was a native. We had salad to start with. Then pork with cheese melted in the middle with green beans. Then we had cake for pudding. The girls had Cola, Martin had a carafe of red wine and I had one of white wine that held enough wine for two glasses. We couldn't believe it. All that for such a low price, and it was lovely.

We did enough shopping to last a couple of days. 'Oh wow, look at those tarts.' Sandra's eyes were popping out of her head.

The tarts were glazed and garnished with all sorts of fruits. We had to try one. After all we are on holiday and it is just fruit.

We had a map from the people that we had booked the cottage with. The place was a little hard to find as all the lanes looked the same, but we found it by about four o'clock that afternoon.

The cottage was beautiful with lots of land for the kids to go wild in; there was a patio with a table and six chairs and a barbecue if we wanted.

We dialled the number of the man who looks after the place to let him know that we had arrived. He reached in few minutes with the key and a box of French goodies that we had paid twenty euros for.

He was a pleasant man about 5 feet 10 inches tall, not very good-looking but not that bad. His name was Mark.

The cottage was spotless with four bedrooms. There was no problem with the sleeping arrangements.

'Mum, can we look in the food box from Mark?' Kerry was yelling.

'If you must, but don't open anything until we have all seen what's in there, OK?' I yelled back.

No answer. Just rustling and banging of tins and packets and the odd 'Wow, look at that.'

'Was that stuff worth the money?' I called. No answer. 'Hey, I'm talking to you lot.'

'Mmm... sorry, love. Yes, it's great,' Martin called.

I was feeling a bit fed up with them munching downstairs and me sorting out the rooms and clothing.

Along with the almost-eaten box of biscuits, there were croissants, jam, butter, French cheese, tea, coffee, milk, sugar, French stick, wine, a bottle of cola, a bag of sweets and, best of all, a small box of chocolates.

'Right, they are for me, seeing that the others ate nearly all the biscuits,' I told myself as I put the things away.

I put the kettle on, and Martin and I set about trying to work the cooker. Once sorted, I put a casserole in to cook. Then we put our coats on and went to sit outside. It was a bit chilly, but we are on holiday so outside we will sit.

'Here we go, happy holiday.' Martin was bringing the wine and Cola out with the remaining biscuits and the sweets.

'I think all this fresh air will make us more hungry,' Sandra said popping another sweet in her mouth.

Martin leaned towards her, 'Don't tell your mother that, she doesn't need any more excuses.' They giggled.

'I'm just going to ignore you,' I grunted. 'Anyway, no one diets or exercises on holiday, before you come up with any more bright ideas.'

By the time dinner was ready, it was too cold to sit out. So we ate inside. By about half past ten, the kids were ready for bed. They were worn out... it had been a long day.

Martin made a cup of tea, and we sat on the sofa in the quiet, just cuddling up and relaxing. 'This is nice, just us two for a while,' Martin smiled. 'Got any more biscuits or something?'

'Well, that killed the romance,' I said as I handed him whatever I could find. Then I went to bed disappointed.

Chapter Five

'Martin, it's ten o'clock, I should be up,' I said.

'Why? This is what holidays are about,' he yawned.

'I know but I want to try one of those croissants.' I was poking him.

'You on about food already? You have only been on a diet not hunger strike, you know.' He was laughing.

The croissants were soft and fluffy, with a lovely buttery taste. The thick spreading of jam I had put on top was sweet and reminded me of summer.

'That looks good,' Kerry wondered. 'It is good.' Kerry went in the kitchen to toast herself a croissant. 'Mmm... this is great.'

By eleven o'clock we had all eaten and were taking showers one by one. The shower was not a very big one as the bathroom itself was small. So it took a while for us all to be ready.

We all bundled into the car ready to go shopping. Twenty minutes later we all climbed out of the car with no shopping.

'Stop moaning, I forgot the shops close for lunch,' I said as everyone was saying it was all my fault.

'I know but you could have remembered before we got to town,' Daisy was going on.

Martin was getting fed up with the girls' continuous moaning. He went to the back of the car and got a football out. He took it to the girls and said, 'There, kick that about. It might stop you moaning so much.'

We found the barbecue and the dustbin to be one set of goal posts. Then we found a garden chair and the sunshade stand for the other set of goal posts. We all played as having two girls to be goalies and only one player was not much fun. So Martin and I joined in.

We had lunch at about two. It was just salad rolls and a nice slice of fruit tart.

We finally got to the town to do the shopping. The supermarket was not huge, but they had a good selection of Easter eggs.

The girls were looking as to which one they would like, 'Can I have this one, pleeeease, Daddy,' Daisy begged. 'OK.' Martin always gives in to her.

'Mum, Mum… ' I looked about to see who was whispering my name. 'Yes, Kerry love, what is it?'

'Mum, can I get this one for Simon? It's only eight euros.' She was very close to me and whispering in my ear so that her dad didn't know what was going on.

We put the egg in the trolley as fast as we could. I didn't look at all the things in the trolley as I was hoping that Martin had got me an egg, and I didn't want to spoil the surprise.

We spent some time in the village looking about. I spent a lot of time with my nose pressed up against shop windows trying to smell the lovely chocolate things on display, and each time one of my family would drag me away shaking their heads or making funny noises at me.

When we got back and unloaded, I could see all the lovely chocolate things in my head. Then I remembered the chocolates I had put in the cupboard out of everyone's way, 'Who wants a cuppa,' I called more loudly than was necessary so no one could hear me taking the wrapper of the box. Great, they all want tea. That gives me more time to try the chocolates.

I looked at that little diagram that informs you what is in each chocolate. It might just as well have been written in double Dutch, I would have understood it just the same. But I decided not to waste anymore time. I binned the paper and stuffed a sweet in my mouth. It was a soft caramel, runny, sweet and so smooth. I savoured the flavour for a while. 'I'm just letting it brew,' I yelled and put another sweet in. I tried to chew it, but it was not good. It was a very hard toffee – not good when you are trying to sneak a sweet while you are making tea.

'What you doing with that tea? It's taking ages. Do you want a hand?' Martin called. 'No, I'm just coming, thanks,' I called back, almost swallowing the sweet whole. I had toffee stuck to my teeth, and it was hard to open my mouth properly as I took the tea in.

I grinned as I put the tray down, a full smile would have shown the sweet stuck around my teeth. I had to wash the sticky toffee off my teeth. So in my wisdom, I took a big mouthful of tea (wisdom is not one of my strong points). The tea was hotter than I had anticipated. It made the toffee stickier. So it was now hot and it stuck to the roof of my mouth (it only took about three days for the blister to go).

We went out to find the restaurant in the village where we had been to earlier, 'Are we going to try something very French, like snails?' Martin was grinning. 'No way,' the kids yelled. I just smiled, as the roof of my mouth was still raw even though I had swilled ice-cold water round it about twenty times.

The restaurant was a nice, little place. It was not too big but not cramped very French looking with old photos on the wall of what the place was like years ago. The tables had a flowery cloth on them and were laid up very smartly.

The waitress was probably about the same age as the building by the looks of her, and like the building she was pleasant. Ordering the meal was a little difficult, but she was patient with us and giggled at our poor attempt at speaking to her in her own language finally we had ordered our food and were enjoying a glass of wine.

We had ordered *pate de tete, which we later found out, was pig's head pate*. We all like pate, so we were happy with it, but it was odd the way the waitress kept grinning at us when we ordered it. It was like she knew something about it that we didn't. It was only pate, so what was she grinning at?

The pate arrived with fresh bread and at least a whole lettuce each and gherkins. The pate had an unusual taste but wasn't too bad. The kids picked at theirs but got through it.

Next we had beef in red wine with carrots and green beans; the beef was so tender you didn't need a knife.

Kerry was looking at me with a strange expression, 'Mum, how do we know this is beef and not horse?'

'Yeah, my teacher says the French eat horse.' Smiled Sandra.

'Thank you for that, you two. I'm sure it's beef, but if your ears start growing then you know I was wrong.' Martin laughed.

'Mum, I was wondering why you had to take a big gulp of your tea when it was you that had just made it?'

'Well, Daisy—Oh, look, pudding. That looks good.' I got out of that one!

The pudding was very lovely. Chocolate mousse, very light but very chocolaty, and the timing was perfect.

Easter Sunday and the kids were up and chattering by 9 o'clock. They get just as excited about Easter as they do about Christmas. 'Happy Easter' sang Sandra as she came into our room with two mugs of coffee. 'Happy Easter, sweetheart. Thank you. We will be up as soon as we drink our coffee,' Martin said taking the cups from her and she ran off back to the telly.

We came down to find the table lay with croissants; juice and handmade Easter name place cards. It looked very nice and tasted even better.

I handed the girls a bag full of Easter eggs each, 'Thanks, Mum. We thought we were only having one egg this year.' Daisy smiled.

'Are you complaining? You have got one egg. One from us, one from auntie Pat, one from nanny and one from auntie Mandy (that's Martins sister). See, so you all got one each.' I laughed.

Martin came over to me and said, 'Close your eyes. I know we said we would not get anything for each other because of this holiday, but I just had to get you something.' I held my eyes closed tight. I could hear bags rustling. My heart was pounding as I had images of all the lovely Easter eggs I had see in the shops. Which one had he got me? Was it the big, beautiful one that I had pointed out to him in hope? It seemed like hours standing there with my eyes closed.

'OK, open you eyes,' Martin was beaming, 'Thank you, it is very big. When did you manage to get that? I have been with you all the time?'

'When we went shopping on Saturday. Remember, I said that Sandra and I had something to look at? We had seen it as we came in the shop so we got it and put it in the car out of your way.'

'Their flowers are done as beautifully as their Easter eggs, don't you think?' Martin was asking me as I placed my Easter egg-shaped bouquet of flowers on the table. They were lovely. The colours were so bright and cheerful, and the ribbon round the middle was a soft pink colour. I stood for a moment to admire them.

'Are you sure you like them? I bet you wish they were chocolate.' Kerry was next to me looking at me like she could read my mind.

'I love them. The way they look like an Easter egg is amazing.' I smiled at her. It was true I did love them, but it was also true that I would have loved them more had they been chocolates, but I was not going to tell any of them that.

'Glad you like them. They are from the girls. This is from me,' Martin was holding out a bag for me to take. I took the bag and looked inside, 'Thank you.' I gave him a big kiss. It was the big egg I had pointed out to him, 'As it is so big, I will share it with you all.'

'Oh good, I was hoping you would say that,' Sandra beamed at me.

We gave Martin his Easter egg and things. His egg was big and he never offered to share his, but still I can't say anything, as I'm not sharing the chocolates in the cupboard.

We had got some small eggs to hide in the garden, and as the garden was so big, Martin and I took half a bag each to hide. I realized that the eggs were about mouth sized as I popped one in. Martin was on his way over to me, 'I've done mine,' he was calling, 'are you eating those eggs?'

'Yes. They are very nice, want one?' I answered trying not to feel guilty.

'Yeah, why not? They have got enough,' he said popping one in his mouth. 'Mmm... they are nice. Keep another couple out for us.'

I looked at him in surprise. '... And you say about me.' I laughed.

The afternoon went well. The girls enjoyed hunting the eggs, and Martin and I enjoyed a bottle of wine while we watched them. The wine helped to keep us warm, you understand.

After they had found all the eggs we went inside to warm up. I opened the egg that I had been given. It was wrapped simply but nicely. As I opened the egg, a large amount of little, hard-shelled eggs fell out. I passed them around for everyone to taste. They all liked them except for me. I had actually found something sweet that I didn't like.

I left the egg alone for later and started on the dinner. I knew it wouldn't matter if it were a bit late. We had all eaten a lot of chocolates today, so a late dinner would be OK.

After I got the dinner on the go and had popped a couple of sweets in my mouth to keep me going as I did dinner, I was getting very good at getting things out of places and into my mouth without making a noise. I went into the front room with a cup of tea for us all. We were lucky that the cottage had a telly, a video player and a DVD player along with a selection of things to watch. It was not a huge selection, but a good one for holidaymakers. We chose a light-hearted comedy.

Dinner was ready about nine o'clock, and it was worth the wait as the beef was tender and the potatoes were crisp. The selection of veg was as Daisy put it – green. The cake we got for pudding was, of course, chocolate with pistachio nut. It was as good to eat as it was to look at, and the added bonus was that it was big enough for two pieces each. Great, you can't get better than that in my eyes.

It was about one o'clock in the morning by the time we all climbed into bed. Martin had been right. This was the best Easter we had had in years, and I thanked him for it.

The rest of the holiday was great. The weather held out for us. We even had good enough days to go to the beach. We found lots of nice, little restaurants to eat in, so that was very nice for me as it meant I did very little cooking. All too soon we only had two days left of our holiday. We were all a bit sad about it.

Daisy came into the bedroom as I was getting dressed, 'Do we have to go home, Mum?'

'Afraid so. I know it's a shame. It's a lovely country, and the people are so nice.' I gave her a hug and hoped that would make her feel better.

We spent the day at a nice, little town that we found. Lucky for us it was market day. There were the usual clothes stalls, music and knick-knacks, but there were people selling ready-made paella. We got some for dinner. Then we got some local made cheese and of course the wine. I don't think I have ever drunk so much wine in all my life.

We found a little café to have lunch in. We had the special of the day, which was not expensive and the good news for me was that you get a lot for your money. We started with salad that seems to be their thing. Then we had steak and chips. It was always too under cooked for the girls, so we spent a lot of time sending theirs back for more cooking, but Martin and I like ours a bit under cooked. We finished our meal with ice cream. I'm not going to tell you what flavour I had.

We got back with our goodies from the market to a lovely, warm evening, so we ate outside. It was seven o'clock but it was still warm. We stayed outside until it got too cold. Then we went in for a cup of tea and see what we could nibble on, in front of the telly.

It was our last whole day left in France. It felt sad to go, but I knew I had to go home and find a job. I got up and dressed, and started to make sure everything was back in its right place before we go tomorrow. I wanted to leave the place as we had found it.

As I got dressed I noticed, as I had for the past few days, that my clothes were getting tight. I had to change my jeans even though they were stretch. All the stretch had been used up and to sit down in them was painful, and to add to it the zip gave up and broke in two never to meet again. I found some elastic-waisted trousers to wear.

For breakfast we just finished off all the leftovers that you could have for breakfast. We sat eating and chatting. Martin was fidgeting a lot. 'My clothes are more than a bit tight,' I told him.

'So are mine. I will have to do something about it when we get home,' he moaned.

Oh no! Panic was upon me. Martin was always good at dieting. He always shows me up. I will have to think of something, so he doesn't lose weight faster than me.

We stayed at the cottage all morning and had lunch there. We finished things off like we had for breakfast except this time we could eat all the lovely chocolate things. It's easy to forget how tight your clothes are and how much weight you have put on when you're in elastic-waisted trousers.

We decided to stay at the cottage for the afternoon. The girls did whatever they felt like. I finished cleaning the place and Martin popped out at about four o'clock that afternoon. He had gone for only about half an hour. He came in holding a white box tied with pink ribbon, 'I thought we should have a nice treat before we go; a nice, fresh cake from the bakers'.' He grinned. Nice was not a good enough word.

We were going to go out for dinner for the last time on our holiday. Mark had been round with our deposit of 200 euro, so we were going to enjoy our last night out. With my elastic trousers on, I was ready to eat for England and France, which was not a problem for me.

We went to a steak house type place. It was nice, the biggest place we had been to in all our holiday.

We had a large starter. It was one that we could all share. It had chicken wings, onion rings, prawns and spare ribs. It was a huge plate of food, but we made light work of it. Next was the main meal. Daisy and Sandra went for the barbeque chicken and chips. Martin had a huge steak with pepper sauce and chips. Kerry and I went for the barbeque ribs. We were glad we had jacket potatoes. They made a nice change. The ribs were so big they were hanging off the plate. As I looked at the ribs I started to wonder how long ago it was since I had been able to feel my ribs, or how long it will be until I could. I put the thought away and tucked into my dinner.

'Are you girls going to be able to eat all that?' Martin asked.

'Yes, no problem,' came the answer.

'Well, let me know if you have a problem with it.'

'One touch of our dinner and you'll be sorry,' the girls warned.

It took us ages to eat our dinner. Kerry and I were in such a mess with all the sticky sauce, we cleaned ourselves up as best we could and sat chatting. As we did, I noticed a man looking at me for long. I was feeling flattered. Maybe I'm not so bad even for my size.

'Mum, Mum… ' Kerry was nudging me. 'I've been trying to tell you that you have got sauce on your chin.'

I was so embarrassed. The man was laughing, and I was so red. How could I think he was eyeing me up? I should have known.

'I was saving that for later,' I said, trying to hide my embarrassment.

We carried on chatting about the holiday and things as we chose the pudding.

'Did you remember to pack the Easter egg you got your boyfriend?' Daisy asked Kerry.

Kerry's glare at Daisy was not unnoticed by Martin, who knew nothing of the egg and wanted to know now.

'Kerry got a little egg for her boyfriend that's all. Nothing to get worked up about. I said she could,' I answered, trying to keep it casual.

'Why didn't you tell me?'

'Because I know how you feel about her having a boyfriend. Look how you reacted when you found out she had one.' I smiled.

'Yeah, but I was being silly. I worry about her.' He grinned.

'Don't worry, Dad. If he creates hassle, I promise to let you know.'

'You better. So when are you bringing him round? Anyway has he got a name?'

Here we go, I thought. Martin will go mad. Kerry looked at me a little unsure what to do. I nodded at her. He had to know sooner or later.

'His name is Simon,' Kerry almost whispered.

'Simon, not simple Simon from the next street?' He looked like thunder.

'Yes, don't be cross. Get to know him first.' She looked like she was going to cry. 'Anyway, he's not simple.'

Martin looked a bit calmer. 'OK, I will meet him then. I will make up my mind. After all everything I've heard about him is only hearsay. I will let you know after I've met him.'

Before we ordered our pudding Martin ordered children's cocktails and cocktails for us. We were thrilled. It was a real treat. By the time I had finished my second cocktail along with the wine we had had with dinner, I was feeling a bit tipsy. Our pudding was a huge ice cream with chocolate pieces, nuts, cream and wafers. It was great and it tasted great. We all had coffee, and Martin and I had brandy to finish a great holiday.

We had been in the restaurant for about 4 hours but it went so fast. By the time we got back to the cottage, my legs were a bit wobbly. Not too bad but enough. We all went to bed as we had an early start the next morning. My legs were glad to be laid in my bed.

It was the first time during the entire holiday that we had used the alarm clock, and now it was ringing very loudly in my head and I was having trouble getting up.

'My head hurts,' I moaned to Martin.

'It's your own fault. Drinking so much when you knew we had an early start.' He was laughing at me.

'I know, don't nag, we had a good evening. I will take some tablets and I will be fine,' I said keeping my fingers crossed.

Martin and the girls found themselves breakfast. I'm sure they were clanging and banging around more this morning. Everything seemed to be a lot louder than normal.

'Do you want some breakfast?' Someone shouted to me. 'No, thank you and please don't shout.'

'Are you OK, Mum?' Sandra was worried. She's always worried when someone was not his or her normal self.

'Don't worry. You're mum is fine, although she would be better if she had not drunk so much last night,' Martin explained.

'But I didn't feel drunk,' I protested.

'It was the mixture of drink that has done it. We had wine, cocktails and brandy. No wonder you have headache.'

I took my large cup of tea to the garden. Maybe the fresh air will help, and anyway I didn't want to listen to Martin going on at me anymore.

We were all ready to be off by eight o'clock. The place was as clean as we had found it. My head was feeling better, and by about ten o'clock I was ready to eat, 'Can we stop at the next service, please. I'm starving.'

'Well, I don't know about that. You should have had breakfast, shouldn't she have, girls?' He laughed as the girls agreed with him.

It was just a few minutes later when we pulled in to the car park of the service station. The others headed for the loos, and I headed for the shop. It was a bit expensive but I was starving. I got the girls and Martin a chocolate bar and myself a large bag of crisps and a chocolate bar. Everyone had a bottle of water as well.

'What have you got there? We didn't get crisps,' said Martin as I munched away.

'I know, but you had breakfast.'

'I'm sure my breakfast was not as big as that bag of crisps. Have you seen this, kids?' He waved the bag at them.

'I told you I was starving, so these will fill me up,' I grunted.

'Suppose you have got a chocolate bar as well? As if I need to ask.'

'Yes, I have the same as you.' I didn't like to tell him that I had a king-size bar. I think that would have been too much for him to take.

'It's taking you a long time to eat that chocolate bar. How many have you got stashed in there?' Martin asked after a while.

'I've got one. I'm making it last by just breaking a bit off at a time. As I'm back on my diet on Monday, I want to make it last as long as I can. What are you lot laughing at?'

'Nothing, Mum.' They giggled.

I knew what they were thinking. So this time I will make a good effort, I promised myself. Besides, I have to beat Martin.

Our ferry was at 12.15 p.m. We booked in at half past eleven and were told to go straight on, as they were loading. I wanted to go home but at the same time I didn't. There didn't seem much to go home to or for. Kerry was leaving school soon, and she would be out of work. I did my best to tell her about trying hard at school, but she wouldn't listen. So now all she has are basic qualifications. Even

Martin's job is not that safe at the moment. The more I thought, the worse I felt about going home.

I snapped myself out of it and told myself it was because we had such a good holiday and the first one in years. It's made me a bit sad about going back.

We wondered around the ferry looking in the duty free shop. We had all gone our separate ways when I heard Martin calling me.

'Look at this. You know that chocolate you had, the one that took you ages to eat? Well, they have got them here… cheaper. We could all have had a king size bar from here.' He was looking at me out the corner of his eye.

'I don't know what you're on about?'

'Don't you? Well, if you didn't drop your wrappers on the car floor then I would not have seen it when I stuffed the camera under your seat.' He was waving the wrapper at me.

'Excuse me, sir, we much prefer our customers to pay for their goods before they eat them,' the security guard told Martin. 'Please be sure to pay for that chocolate bar at the till.' He walked away before Martin could tell him the truth.

'That will teach you. Are we getting anything from here? Some of that wine we like, maybe the red to match your face?' I laughed at him.

Martin sulked for the rest of the trip back to England and kept muttering about how he never got a chance to explain and how it was all my fault, but I told him that you never wave an empty packet in a shop where they sell the same. He just grunted at me.

We came into port and still had a long way to go. We stopped at a fish and chip shop. I loved the French food, but you can't beat good old fish and chips, and seeing as we were sort of still on holiday, my diet had not started yet.

We had forgotten about all the traffic. It seemed to take forever to get home. We finally got home at about seven that night. It had been a long day. We plonked our things in the dinning room, half because we were tired and half because we didn't want to be home.

'I'm glad it's Saturday. I'm not getting up till midday,' Daisy was tired and so she was moaning.

Kerry made a cup of tea only because she wanted to call Simon to tell him she was back. An hour later we had to shout to her to get off the phone. It would have been cheaper to have gone round his house.

Martin and I counted out what money we had left. We had got rid of all our euros and still had a good amount left in pounds. There was nothing to eat in the house. We will need to go shopping, but not tonight.

About twenty minutes later the front door bell rang, 'Three large pizzas and four garlic breads,' the delivery boy said. Martin paid, and we waited at the table. It didn't take long before the boxes were empty. It was very nice. I didn't realize how hungry I was but then it was half past eight and we had had fish and chips at about two that afternoon. No wonder we were hungry. As if I need an excuse.

We went to bed at about ten. We were very tired. We still chatted for ages about the holiday. I was still feeling sad that it was over.

Saturday and I must weigh myself. This is something I didn't want to do. I got the scales out and put them on the kitchen floor (that is, the flattest floor in the house). I closed my eyes and stepped on.

'Ha ha ha. You did make a pig of yourself, didn't you?' Martin laughed down my ear. 'You weigh 85.3 kilograms. Well, what are you going to do about that, fatty?'

'OK, mister slim, you get on. Ha ha… 96.4 kilograms! Now who's been a pig?' I was so cross.

'Don't get stressed. We all overdid it. That's what holidays are for.' He was trying to creep round me and give me a big hug.

'I will shift mine in a month.' He smiled.

'I will shift mine in a month,' I mimicked. 'Not if I have anything to do with it.'

Chapter Six

We went shopping with what money we had left. As we paid, I noticed that there was a notice board. Pinned to it was an advertisement for jobs going at the supermarket itself. To apply there were instructions to go to customer service. So off I went. The lady gave me an application form to fill and told me that they would phone me if I was lucky.

At home I told the girls about the job. 'What job did you apply for?' asked Sandra.

'The Checkout, That way I can't eat all day. Then I will beat your father at losing weight.' I grinned.

'Oh, a challenge, is it? That's good. I'm up for that.'

Great. I should have kept my mouth shut. Will I ever learn? We unpacked the shopping. There was not much. Not only did we not have a great deal of money, we also didn't buy a lot of sweet things, so that cut our shopping by about half.

'I could murder a couple of biscuits to go with this cup of tea.' Martin was looking in his cup.

'So could I.' I was thinking how we always had biscuits with our drink on the holiday, and now it's a habit.

It was getting a bit mad in our house with the washing machine going, the housework to see to and then in the midst of it all the doorbell rang. Then Daisy and Kerry started on each other. It appeared that Simon was at the doorstep, and Daisy had called Kerry in a silly voice just to embarrass her.

I looked at Martin whose expression had changed. 'Don't start. You promised to give him a chance. I bet he is very nervous. Anyway, I've met him. He seems OK.'

'When did you meet him? You never said.'

'I was in town, and I saw them together so I went over and spoke to them. Do I have to tell you everything?'

I had opted out of telling him that. I was coming out of the baker's with a big, fat iced-ring doughnut when I had seen them.

Kerry showed Simon into the front room where we had just sat down to another cup of tea. Simon looked very nervous and so did Kerry, 'Dad, this is Simon. Simon, this is my dad, Martin.' She grinned the best she could.

Martin and Simon greeted each other with a handshake. Not that Simon needed to; he was shaking enough already.

I smiled at Simon as we greeted, and I offered him coffee. Kerry and I left the men alone to get on while we made the drinks.

'Do you think Dad will be nice to him?' She was wringing her hands.

'Don't worry. Your dad is not that bad. Anyway, he knows I will sort him out if he is not.' I laughed.

'Oh, I didn't get any biscuits when I went shopping. What on earth can I offer to go with the coffee?'

'We have some left from the holiday. I put them at the back of the cupboard so you didn't eat them all.' She grinned cheekily.

'You are a good girl... sometimes.' I winked at her.

Kerry and I went into the front room slowly so we could hear what was being said. We could hear laughing. We looked at each other. I looked at the plate and noticed that there was only one of my favourite biscuits left. What was I going to do? I had to think fast. 'Kerry, can you take the tray a minute?' As she took it, my hand flashed out, and I grabbed the biscuit. I stuffed it in my mouth whole and took the tray from Kerry.

Kerry just stood there staring at me, then laughed.

'You should have seen what Mum just did.' Kerry told the men all about it.

'Why does that not surprise me?' Martin was grinning.

Simon was unsure whether to laugh. I bet his mum never did things like that. I bet she is all thin and good with her eating.

Martin and Simon had got on well. Martin had asked a lot of questions, and I knew he would. He seemed pleased with the answers. Simon had come round to tell Kerry that he had just got a job as a mechanic but will still go to college one day a week for a while. Martin was pleased that at least he was not lazy. Martin had also quizzed him about the bad things he had heard about him. Again Martin was pleased with the answers, and he warned Simon that as long as he kept out of trouble he was welcome. However, as soon as he got in trouble again, he was never to knock on Martin's door. A few tense minutes passed, but all was agreed and everyone relaxed.

Kerry gave Simon his egg, and I was willing him to open it and offer it around. He didn't as he was going to take it home to show his mum, 'what a wimp. Must be a mummy's boy.' I thought to myself, but I was being unkind and I did feel bad about it. After all the egg was his, and he did the right thing taking it home to show his mum. It was only because I wanted some chocolate that I was being unkind.

Lunch was late. As usual I was getting good at doing lunch and dinner late. We had ham rolls and yoghurts. Simon went home while we still ate as he had eaten at the right time. After we had eaten, Kerry went to Simon's. I told her to be back before eight, or if she was eating at Simon's she should let me know. Then she was gone.

About ten minutes later there was a knock at the door. It was the twins from three doors down. They go to school with Daisy and came round to see if Daisy and Sandra would like to watch a new DVD with them and then have some dinner.

'Can we go, Dad?' asked Daisy looking up at him, all cute.

'Yes, you can go, but be good and call when you want to come home. I will come and get you.'

'Dad, it's only three doors away and I'm nearly 14. I'm sure we can walk that far on our own,' Sandra said.

'OK but run,' he shouted after them.

'That was Kerry on the phone. She is staying at Simon's for dinner and will be in about half past ten. He is going to walk her home. Martin informed me as he came into the kitchen.

'OK, Just us two to have dinner. What do you want?' I asked.

'Well, seeing as you're asking...' He said pulling me to him and winking.

'For dinner.' I laughed.

'I was talking about dinner. I was thinking of takeaway chicken followed by a box of chocolates for two. Don't know what you were thinking.'

'That sounds great. Can't wait for dinner. Why were you pulling me to you then?'

'Because my little cherub you have the money, and I will need it to get the dinner.' He grinned.

Martin cleaned out the car and busied about the house making sure everything was ready for school on Monday. At about half past seven Martin went out for our dinner; he came back with a bargain box.

'That's a lot for two.' I looked at the box.

'Well, I don't know about you, but I'm starving. That roll was not very filling, and it was nearly 5 hours ago.'

We didn't bother with plates. We took the food from the box. It always seems to taste better that way. Martin opened a bottle of wine that we had got from the duty free and poured us a large glass each. We had just finished our first bit of the chicken when we thought we heard a noise. We looked at each other, shook our heads, took a gulp of wine and went in for our second bit of chicken. 'So that's what you do when we are not here.' Sandra was looking at our box.

'What are you doing here?' I asked in disbelief. I didn't mean to sound disappointed that they were home. It's just that we don't often get time on our own.

'One of the twins was sick and had to go to bed. She has come down with something, so we said we would go home,' they explained.

'You have had dinner though, haven't you?' Martin asked hopefully.

'No, we are starving. Is there enough for us?'

'Yes, of course. Your dad must have known this would happen. That's why he got the biggest box.' I smiled.

'Where's the plates?' asked Sandra.

'We are not having plates; we are being like lazy teenagers eating in the front room with no plates,' Martin told her.

'Can you remember that far back?' Laughed Daisy as she pulled a bit of chicken from the box.

'Yes, you cheeky mare,' Martin laughed as he snatched her bit of meat from her hand and ate it.

'Daaad...' she said, getting another bit.

We went to bed at about 11.45 p.m. We had a good evening, even with the kids coming home. We had watched a film and had a laugh with them. Martin opened the box of chocolates; 'We don't have to share everything with the kids.' He grinned. We ate the lot. I did start to feel a bit sick but that soon passed.

Sunday and it was a lovely, sunny Sunday, but then it was the end of April too. Well, nearly just a couple of days to go. Martin was up and I could smell breakfast cooking, so up I got and off I went following the smell. As I neared the dining room, I could hear voices. The kids must be up, but that was a man's voice, I'm sure. I sneaked into the dining room to find Martin and Simon eating sausage, egg, bacon, beans and toast.

'Morning,' I said extra loud in the hope that Martin would jump up to get my breakfast.

'Morning, love, want a cup of tea?' Martin was smiling. Well, of course he was smiling. So would I have been if I had that lot in front of me.

'Yes, please,' I said looking from his plate to him in the hope that he might get the hint.

'You don't mind me having breakfast, do you, Mrs. Kerry's mum?' Simon looked like he had been caught out. That was more than how Martin had reacted.

I wanted to say, 'Yes, I do mind. That would have been mine if you weren't here,' but I couldn't. I replied, 'No, of course not. You tuck in, and my name is Alice, not Mrs. Kerry's mum.' I smiled as sweetly as I could.

'Sorry,' he blushed.

'No worries. So darling husband of mine, where is my breakfast?'

'I didn't think you would want any after all the chocolates you ate last night,' he called from the kitchen.

'You cheeky sod. You ate half,' I retorted.

He came in with my tea and a plate. 'Thank you, I will take it all back.' I smiled at him as I took the cup and plate.

'No, I won't. How come I only get toast?'

Martin went back into the kitchen for the sauce. He came back and sat down 'Who's eaten one of my sausages and dunked it in my egg?'

I dunked the last bit of sausage in his egg again and said 'I don't know who would do such a thing.'

We were all laughing when the girls came down to see what all the noise was about. 'Your dad is doing teas and breakfast.' I smiled at him sweetly.

Simon told Kerry about the breakfast. 'They are like a couple of kids,' he finished.

'They have been like that since the holiday. I think it was the fresh air; it's leaked into their brains. Simon why are you here? Not that it's not nice to see you but why?' She looked puzzled.

'There was a fire at our house last night... well, this morning about 4 o'clock. It is quite badly damaged,' he explained.

'Is your mum OK?' I had heard that his mum and dad were divorced and that she had struggled to bring him, his brother and sister up on her own.

'Yes, she is OK. My mum and my sister are in hospital. They are keeping them in to keep an eye on them because of smoke and stuff.'

'Where was your brother?' I asked.

'He doesn't live at home. He moved out about six weeks ago. He lives in a flat with his girlfriend.'

'Where were you?' asked Kerry.

'I was at David's. After I got back from walking you home, the phone rang. It was David. He asked if I would help him with his car. He said he needed it for today. He had been working on it all day and was getting nowhere. So went to help. His mum said that I could sleep on the sofa, as it was too late to go home. Then their phone rang. It was our neighbour who called to say my house was on fire. I'm glad I told Mum where I was, or she might have thought that I was still in the house trapped or something and tried to save me. I'm trying to make things up to Mum. You know… for all the trouble I have caused her.' He looked sad with the memories coming back.

'Are you going to see them this morning?' I tried to sound cheery.

'Yes, Martin said he would drop me off. Hope I'm not being a nuisance. Is it OK if Kerry comes?' he asked.

'No, you not being a nuisance; and yes, she can, if you're sure your mum wont mind,' I said.

'No, she won't. She really likes Kerry. We can get the bus back.'

'OK, no problem. Dinner is about three o'clock, if you want some.'

We had a lazy day and in the afternoon I put the dinner in to cook. Then we sat in the garden to enjoy the sunshine. I had put some crisps in a bowl, so we can all munch on them. I don't know why I put them in a bowl. I always eat more when I do that.

I was enjoying the sunshine and was so engrossed in my book that I forgot about the dinner in the oven until I smelt something burning. Then I jumped up and ran to the kitchen, but I was too late. The dinner was burnt. The saucepans would never be the same again. I got as much of the burnt dinner off as I could, but one saucepan had to go in the bin along with its contents. I went into the garden and said, 'Seeing as it's such a nice day, I thought chicken salad would be good.' I smiled.

'What happened to the roast you were going to do,' Kerry asked as she came in with Simon.

'Give you three guesses… ' Daisy said pointing at me.

'You ate the roast.' Kerry looked at me.

'No, I didn't. What a thing to say. I burnt it. I forgot about it as I was reading.'

Half an hour later we sat down to a lovely salad. In fact it was nicer than the roast would have been, even before I burnt it.

'What's for pudding? Hope it's something good as we start our diet tomorrow,' Martin asked.

I glared at him. Why did he have to say that in front of everyone?

'What? Was I not supposed to say anything?' He looked puzzled.

We got through a large apple pie and 2 litres of custard for pudding. Simon explained that his mum and sister were coming out of the hospital tomorrow, and they were all going to stay at his uncle's some 3 miles away. You would have thought he was going 100 miles away from the way Kerry took the news.

As I got into bed I was thinking about the start of yet another diet. Why can't I ever stick to it? Why do I always fail? Maybe I'm destined to be fat.

It was Monday already and time to get up, 'I'm not weighing myself today.' I was talking to myself already.

I slumped into the kitchen, dug out the tins of diet drink and made one. After all the lovely food and drink I had had, this was without doubt disgusting beyond believe, but I gritted my teeth and drank it as fast as possible.

'The only good thing about this drink is that you don't get a lot of mess to clear up preparing them, and in two minutes it's gone,' I moaned to Martin. 'Do you want me to make you one?'

'Yeah, go on. Then I'll give it a go.'

Good, this will sort him out when he tastes just how horrible they are. He won't be so clever about dieting.

'I like this. There is a lot of flavour. Will you do me one for lunch?'

He has got to be joking. How can he like them? This means he will beat me easily. I need a plan and I need one fast.

The kids munched on toast with great dollops of jam on top. I couldn't even look at it so I made myself busy.

They had all gone to wherever they were going to, and I was alone. I must admit it was nice to be alone for a while. It gave me time to work on my plan to beat Martin at dieting. I was so busy that all of a sudden it was lunchtime, and I hadn't eaten a thing since breakfast. For once I had not even thought about eating anything, but I know that wouldn't last.

Martin and I had the milkshake thing. He was sipping his happily, and I was gulping it down to get rid of it. Martin looked at me, 'Why do you have these if you hate them so much?'

'I keep hoping I will get used to them and lose weight. I'm not in tonight. I'm going to the gym with Pat. Is that OK?'

'Yeah, of course it is. Tell you what, while you're there ask to see if there is room for me to join.'

'OK,' I said with no intention of asking. I couldn't have him there. He will see how bad I am, and how I puff like an old steam train… no, no way was I going to ask.

I was busy cleaning the house when the phone rang. It was Pat. She unwell and couldn't go tonight, so we will have to go next week, 'It's probably because she is so thin. That's why she is always ill,' I told myself.

Everyone was home again. The kids were doing homework, Martin was reading the paper and as for me I was sorting the dinner, peeling potatoes and veg, and wishing I had gone out tonight even to the gym.

About seven o'clock I yelled to my lazy lot that dinner was ready. They sat down to the normal 'what we got' question.

'You have pork chops with creamy bacon sauce, mash and veg tonight,' I told them as I handed the dinner out.

'That sounds and looks great,' the kids said.

'That sounds fattening,' replied Martin.

I sat down with my dinner. 'That's not what we have got, what have you got?' asked Sandra.

'I have got baked veg with bacon pieces on top.'

'That's not fair. I've got all this, and you get baked veg, why?' Martin asked.

'Because you go to work and I don't. So you need a proper dinner at night. You only had two milkshakes all day.' I smiled.

'I suppose so.'

My plan was working. All the time I can do this kind of food for him and low fat for me then I'm bound to win.

The dinner was a big hit. At half past ten, all the kids were in bed. Martin and I had a cup of tea and a chat about whatever. We went to bed happy.

The rest of the week was very much the same. I managed to do lots of nice dinners. They had chicken in wine and cream sauce one night, and toad-in-the-hole another night. This is how it went on, but I was having salad or baked veg. I had been good all week and my clothes were not so tight, thank heavens.

Friday night and Kerry was at Simon's uncles for dinner. So it was just the four of us for dinner. Martin suggested pizza and chips. Well, the kids were up for that. I knew what he was up to. He knows how much I love chips, but I will show him.

I cooked the chips. The smell was lovely. It was a real test not to cook any for myself. I put the chips in a bowl so that they could help themselves, but I had done a few too many so I put them on a little plate. In the week I had got some diet ready meals that would go in the microwave. So I popped one in, and then took the bowl of chips and the pizzas into the dining room. As I waited for my dinner to be done, the spare chips kept jumping up at me. I took one just to try. They were great, golden and crisp. By the time my dinner was ready I had eaten the spare chips, but there were only six of them, or was it twenty-six. I can't remember.

I sat at the table with my dinner and everyone looked at me.

'Why haven't you got chips?' asked Sandra.

'I didn't want chips.'

'Why did you do them then?' asked Martin

'You and the girls wanted them.'

'I thought you would like chips for a change. You shouldn't have done them just for us.'

'It's OK, I don't mind, if I have lost enough weight tomorrow then I might have a treat.' I could see Martin was not happy about him having chips and not me.

By the time it was bedtime I was starving, but I was not going to give in. I didn't know I would sleep being hungry, but I will have to try.

Saturday morning, and I found myself asking my cup if I should weigh in or not.

'Have you weighed yourself, yet?' Martin was up and getting the scales out.

'No, I don't know whether or not to.'

'Come on, you might surprise yourself,' he said, getting on the scales. 'Hey, 94 kilograms. That's good.' He was happy. He had done well seeing as some of his dinners were not very slimming.

'Come on, your turn,' he said pushing me onto the scales.

' OK, OK, don't push.' I slowly looked at the flashing numbers. 'Yes, 81.6 kilograms. I don't believe it.' I was so happy, I felt like I was getting somewhere.

Martin and I had a milkshake for breakfast and talked about how we could lose more weight next week without the diet getting boring.

I was amazed at how easy it was to talk to him about dieting after all these years. I didn't know he would understand, but that doesn't mean that he can come to the gym with me.

The supermarket was packed with everyone getting things for a barbeque.

'Do you fancy a barbeque tonight?' Martin asked as he looked at the steaks.

'Why not? Better get enough just in case Simon stays. He might be thin, but boy can he eat.'

We were good with our shopping. Lots of healthy things and lots of nice things for the barbeque, and a little bit of bad things for pudding and some wine.

'I'm so hungry. I feel sick,' I told Martin.

'Me too but then it is three o'clock, and all we have had is a milkshake all day.'

We took our shopping out to the car to pack it. We could smell the chips from the McDonald's next door. We looked at each other and knew what each was thinking. Without a word we got ourselves and the shopping in the car and drove to the drive through. It was heaven.

When we got home, Kerry and Simon were cuddled up on the sofa, and the other two were doing their homework. 'Have you had lunch?' I asked.

'Yes, thanks.'

'We are having barbeque tonight. Is that OK?' Martin shouted.

'Yeah, great. Can we have barbecue sauce on the chicken? Have we got something yummy for pudding?' The questions were flying at us from all directions.

'Yes and yes. Simon, are you staying for dinner?' Martin was putting the kettle on.

'Yes, if you don't mind. I love barbeques.'

'Oh lord; I hope we have enough if he loves barbecue. Then we could be in trouble.' I laughed.

We all set about getting things ready for the barbecue. The girls and I made salads and things while Martin and Simon tried to light the barbecue while sipping beer, normal man things.

'That barbecue smells good. Can we start cooking yet? I'm starving,' Simon said. 'I think you both have lost weight. I hope you don't mind me saying.' Simon looked uneasy.

'No, we don't mind at all. We have been trying to diet and we have lost a bit. Thank you.' I smiled.

'Well, I'm not dieting tonight,' Martin said pouring the wine, 'anyway I'm sure I read somewhere that barbecues are good for you. Not sure about the drink, but tonight I don't care.'

Soon we were tucking into the food and drink. I let the girls have wine and lemonade while Simon, Martin and I had wine and whatever else we wanted. Simon had two glasses of wine. Martin and I had two bottles.

We had a choice of pudding. There was trifle or strawberry cheesecake. I was having a problem choosing so I had some of each that solved the problem.

Kerry made coffee and I put little, thin mint chocolates on a plate to share. It was four for the plate and one for Alice.

'Mum, there wont be any left at this rate.' Kerry took the box from me.

'I know, I just love them. Don't tell your dad.' I didn't tell her that the supermarket were offering 'Buy one, get one free.' So there was another box in the cupboard.

It was about midnight before we got to bed. We made a bed up on the sofa for Simon, as none of us were sober enough to take him home. Martin told him he was only to move off the sofa if he needed a drink or the loo. He was not to be sneaking off to rooms where he shouldn't be. By the time we got up next morning Simon was gone.

'You frightened him away,' I told Martin.

'No, he didn't. Simon understood where Dad was coming from and said he would have said the same thing if he was Dad,' explained Kerry. 'Anyway, they are moving back into their house today.

I made Martin and myself a cup of tea and a milkshake for breakfast. 'Is that it?' Martin looked at me.

'I thought you like them. Anyway, you only get one bad day now and again.'

'You're right. We don't want to ruin all our hard work.'

By about eleven o'clock I was hungry (I know that's nothing unusual for me). There was no way I could hold out till lunch. Everyone was busy with whatever. No one was anywhere near me. I opened the box of mint chocolates and took a few out (well, six actually) and started nibbling at one.

'Mum, where are you? Can I have a drink?' Daisy was on her way. I threw the box back in the cupboard and held the chocolates tight in my hand so she couldn't see them.

'I'm in the kitchen,' I called as I sucked the chocolate off my teeth.

'Can I have some orange juice, please?'

'Yes, there are some cartons in the fridge.'

'You smell like mint.' She was screwing her nose up.

'Oh yes, that's because I've just cleaned my teeth.'

She seemed to except this and wondered off to the garden. That was a close one. I will have to be more careful. I opened my hand to eat the chocolates, but they were one melted mess. So I licked it all off my hand and very nice it was too.

I didn't bother to do lunch seeing as everybody had been picking at things all day. I didn't see the point in doing any. I didn't feel like doing a roast so I did shepherd's pie, peas and carrots followed by fruit that I cut up and placed on a large plate for everyone to help themselves.

We had our dinner at about three o'clock. So it left me time to iron the school things and sing to myself as I did so. 'Do you have to sing, Mum?' Sandra asked as she went past me eating little mint chocolates.

'Where did you get them from?' I looked at her horrified.

'I found them in the cupboard. They were already open.'

'Don't eat too many. They are for if anyone comes to visit,' I lied. Now I am going to have to find another place to hide them.

We all felt a bit hungry. So for tea we all had beans on toast. It was a nice change and not too heavy before bed. So I felt happy with myself as I cuddled down to sleep.

Monday morning, what is it about Monday mornings? Even if you don't have to go to work you still get the Monday morning feeling. It's very odd.

'Finally, everyone gone and I'm alone. Right, I'm going to clean out the drawers in my bedside table. Don't know the last time I did them.' I was talking to myself again.

I started by pulling everything out and putting it on the bed. I don't why I do that because I look at it all and wish I had never started the job. 'Oh, I forgot about you.' I was talking to a little white box with a picture of flowers on it. I opened the lid and popped a chocolate in my mouth. It was a lovely, creamy toffee, a bit hard to chew but still lovely. Why is it that when you are eating things you shouldn't be, especially the sticky things, the phone rings? My phone was ringing. I answered sounding like a Teletubbie trying to say hello.

'Hello,' a polite but somewhat puzzled voice answered. 'Can I speak to Mrs Alice Andrews, please?'

'Yes, speaking,' I said, glad that at last I could. We spoke for a few moments. She sounded like a very nice and happy person.

The phone call cheered me up, so I had two more chocolates and finished cleaning out the bedside table.

Martin came home for lunch. It would have been better if he had not. He was unusually quiet. We drank our milkshakes in silence. 'Are you OK?' I asked.

'Yes fine, thanks.' He sort of smiled, then got up and went back to work.

The girls came home as loud and chattering as normal. Martin came home as quietly as at lunchtime. Everyone noticed.

Who Wants to Diet Anyway?

The girls did their homework just to keep out of the way. The atmosphere was not good at all, and we ate our dinner in almost silence. If it hadn't been for Kerry telling us that she will be leaving school next holidays, we would have remained silent.

'That's the end of the month,' I nearly choked. I couldn't believe it.

'So what are you going to do with your life?' Martin asked.

'I don't know. I only have basic qualifications, and the grades on them are not that good.' She looked at the table rather than her dad.

'Well, you wouldn't listen. So now you will just have to get on with it and see what you can get,' he was still grumpy and his tone was not kind.

We all finished our dinner, and with no one – not even me – wanting pudding, we all left the table. I was clearing it when Kerry came back in. She looked like she had been crying. 'Mum, what's wrong with dad?'

'I don't know, love, but I intend to find out.'

In bed I felt the need of a sugar fix. I got the chocolates out the drawer and ate one. Martin came in from the bathroom as I popped another in my mouth, 'What are you eating now?' His voice harsh and unkind.

'My chocolates from Mother's day. I forgot I had them. That's not like me,' I said trying to cheer him up.

'No, that's not like you. I'm surprised you didn't open it that morning and stuff them all in one go.'

'How dare you be so unkind? You're not exactly in yourself?'

'No, but I do try harder than you. You are always sneaking things,' he shouted.

'What is wrong with you?' I shouted back.

'It looks like I'm sure to lose my job,' he was shouting.

'So why didn't you tell me and don't take it out on us. It's not our fault. I didn't do that to you.'

'I know you didn't,' he said as he got into bed. We turned our backs on each other and pretended to go to sleep.

Chapter Seven

I was up early and drinking tea when Martin came down. He looked like he had had about as much sleep as I had, and that was very little. We grunted at each other. We all ate breakfast in the same atmosphere as we had eaten dinner. At last they were all gone out the door, so now I could get myself ready. I put on a bit of make up and went out.

I sat there waiting with butterflies in my tummy and sweaty palms.

'Mrs. Andrews?' A voice called.

'Yes,' I said as I stood up and straightened my skirt.

'Hello, I'm Elizabeth Mann. We spoke on the phone.' She had a warm smile as she showed me in to her office.

Half an hour later we were shaking hands. I went home, kicked of my shoes, and had a cup of tea and the rest of my chocolates. I needed the sugar after my interview. 'There, Mr Goody-goody Martin, now I have stuffed all my chocolates,' I said to the box as I put it in the bin.

My mood lifted, and I was smiling again. I hadn't got the job I had applied for, but I did get a job at the supermarket. That made me feel better. No more being stuck in here with the cleaning and eating.

No one came home for lunch, so I didn't bother with any. Anyway, the chocolate had made me feel bloated and a bit sick.

I was singing away cleaning the bathroom (I have to sing when cleaning. It's the only thing that gets me through it all) when I heard the front door open, then close. I looked at my watch. It was too early for the girls to be home.

'Where are you?' Martin called.

'In the bathroom,' I called back, forgetting to be cross with him.

'Will you be long?'

'I'm just coming.'

I went downstairs to find Martin in the hallway holding a bunch of flowers and a box of chocolates. 'I just wanted to say sorry.'

'Thank you,' I said, taking the gifts. I was not going to say, 'Never mind, it doesn't matter,' because it did matter. What he said to me was very hurtful. I did notice he had a bunch of flowers for Kerry too. That would cheer her up.

We sat and spoke for ages, and before we knew it, the girls were home. Then it all started again, homework, dinner, et cetera. Kerry was very happy with her flowers and gave Martin a big hug.

'OK, come and get it,' I yelled.

'Corr steak and chips. It's like being on holiday again.' Daisy was beaming.

'Is there a reason why we have steak tonight? 'Kerry asked.

'Yes.'

'Well, what's the reason?' asked Martin.

'I got a job.'

'What, when, where, how?' The questions were coming from all directions.

'OK, I had an interview this morning at the supermarket. The job I wanted had gone, but they offered me another job and I accepted it.'

'Why didn't you tell me?' Martin asked.

'Just in case I didn't get the job... anyway, it's hard to tell someone something when you're not talking to them.'

'Well done, Mum. What you going to be doing?'

'Hot chicken and pizza counters.'

'Oh well, there goes your diet then,' said Kerry.

'Thanks for the vote of confidence. My diet will still be on.'

'I bet you will be nibbling on all sorts of things, and before you know what's happened, all your hard work will be gone,' she said matter of factly.

'Well, I will try not too. You see I didn't have chips tonight.' I held my plate up for her to see.

'When do you start?' asked Sandra.

'Monday morning. I might have to work late some weekends. Hope you lot don't mind.'

Everyone seemed OK about the weekends and said they would come and say hello when they are doing the shopping. I have never worked on a Saturday before, but I know how busy it gets. I shop there.

The rest of the week was gone in a flash. The weather was good, so I was able to keep up with the gardening. It stopped me from eating. We had had so much salad this week, I was sure I would turn into a rabbit by June.

Saturday morning and time to weigh in. Here goes... I have been so good this week I must have lost something.

I was singing as I made my milkshake. I had a bit of chocolate left and a bit of vanilla, so I mixed the two together. It was not too bad.

'Are you feeling alright?' Martin was looking at me in a strange way as he put the kettle on.

'Yes, I'm fine. Thanks. Are you going to weigh yourself this morning?'

'Suppose I should, well... that's not bad... 94 kilograms.' He looked pleased.

'Well done. I'm down to 79 kilograms. Hold on... you were 94 kilograms last week.'

'That's great. You do look better for losing the weight.'

'Don't creep round me. You normally do better than me. What's gone wrong?'

'OK, I confess. The milkshakes are not very filling, so on my way back to work I stop at that nice baker's on the corner and get a meat pie and a cake.'

'You should have said. You don't have to have the milkshake.'

'I was trying to make it look good for your sake.'

We left the kids going wherever and eating whatever and we went shopping.

Martin didn't feel like shopping, so he went to the D.I.Y. shop next door. I was glad he went there, so now I could go into the café and have a coffee on my own. The only problem with supermarkets that have cafes is that they do food.

I waited in the long line praying that I wouldn't see anyone I knew. 'Can I help you?' the young girl asked.

'Yes, a coffee, please and a full breakfast.' I replied.

I sat down with my plate. It was full and looking great. I had sausage, egg, bacon, mushrooms and toast. While I was wrestling with my conscience, I dunked the toast into the egg and took a big bite.

'Caught you,' a voice rang out; I nearly fell off my chair.

'Oh Abbey! It's you. You gave me a fright. I thought you were Martin.'

'Can I join you? Did you have a nice holiday? You look like you have lost weight.' Abbey sat down with her breakfast.

'We had a great holiday, and yes, I have lost weight and I was doing well until I came in here.'

'Don't. I work here. Depending on what shift you are doing and what you can get to eat, and seeing as we only pay half price, it's mad. The evening shift is best. You get loads to eat, that's my best shift.' She laughed.

'Did you have to tell me that? I start work here on Monday.'

'That's great. What you doing?'

'Hot chicken and pizza.'

'Those are my counters. We are going to have such fun.' Her eyes were sparkling with mischief.

The young girl cleared our things for us and got us another coffee only because she was Abbey's friend.

'Have you done the shopping, or have you been chatting all this time?' Martin had appeared.

'I'm going to get a cuppa. Want a cake?' Martin was asking us.

'No, thanks,' I answered.

'No, thank you. We are full up from our…' I quickly gave Abbey a kick under the table, '… from our coffees… we have had two.'

'That hurt... aren't you going to tell him about your breakfast?'

'You must be joking... the way he nags.' We sat giggling.

We said bye to Abbey and went shopping. We got home to find that Kerry was out with Simon, and the other two were sitting waiting to see what yummy things we had got. Martin gave them the sweets that we had got them. Then they filled the fruit bowl up for me.

'Oh no, not again. Don't know why mum buys all this fruit. We only throw it way in a weeks time,' Daisy was moaning.

'I know but she thinks it helps her diet and ours, ' Sandra explained.

'Why is it that when mum is on a diet then we are all on a diet?' asked Daisy

'Don't know... maybe, that's just what mums do.'

Martin and I had been listening to them and giggling our heads off. They sounded like a couple of old women.

'Mum, auntie Pat called. Can you call her before five tonight?' Daisy can half shout when she wants to.

I called Pat to see what she wanted. We are going to the gym on Monday. I know my first day back to work... yes... I'm mad.

'I'm going for a bath before dinner. Your dad is cooking. Then if you're lucky, we might have some chocolates later.'

'Does dad have to cook... I mean... it's OK, but... ' Sandra was moaning.

'Thanks a lot. You could go hungry,' he said.

'Mum, you remember the chocolates that you had for Mother's day? Could we have some tonight?' asked Daisy.

'I don't know... I will think about it... they are special, you know... shut up, Martin.' He had started to laugh.

Martin did a nice dinner. It was spicy chicken in those pancake wrap things. They were lovely, even the kids ate them.

'Mum, Kerry's on the phone,' Daisy was yelling.

'I will talk to her. Your mother is eating... ' 'Martin went to the phone.

I could hear him saying 'OK' and 'That's fine' and 'be careful' and 'tell him to look after you.' Then he came back into the dining room.

'Kerry is staying at Simon's tonight. It's his uncle's birthday, and they are going out to dinner.'

'She hasn't got any money,' I said.

'That's OK. They are going to pop in here first. How much have you got?'

'Not a lot… ' I said as I looked in my purse.

Kerry and Simon rushed in and out again. They were running late, nothing unusual for Kerry.

'We can open these chocolates that your dad got me." I said

'What about the ones I got you?' asked Daisy.

'OK, I confess. I have eaten them and very nice they were too.'

'You said you would share them.'

'I know, I'm sorry. You were at school, and I just couldn't stop eating them. They were so lovely.'

'That's OK. They were yours and as long as they were nice. But to make up for it, I get to choose first tonight.'

'You are a terror.' Laughed as I handed her the box.

Chapter Eight

Sunday and I was not getting up yet. This is going to be my last lay in for a while, and I'm going to make the most of it.

'Are you getting up, sleepy head?' Martin came in the room.

'Yes, at some point today, I will get up.'

'That's good to know. I'm going to cut the grass. The kids are in the garden messing around with their phones, so there goes their credit,' he walked muttering something about lazing in bed.

I pushed the covers off myself. 'Come on, Alice, get your backside out of bed,' I told myself. I took my tea into the garden and hoped I could find some energy.

'You missed breakfast, Mum. It's nearly lunchtime.' Sandra laughed.

'That's OK. I'm sure I can still fit breakfast in somewhere in the day.'

I had everything ready for school, so I was planning a lazy day and a lazy day I had. All I did was cook dinner and load the dishwasher. Kerry came home in a weird mood. She was acting strange. Well, more strange than normal for a teenager. So that's very strange.

'Hi, sweetheart. You OK?' I asked.

'Yes, I'm fine. Can Simon come round this evening?'

'Of course he can. Have you had a row?'

'No, we had a great time. His family are very nice.' She had an odd smile on her.

Simon came round about six o'clock that evening. I could hear them in the hallway. Simon was sort of whispering, 'Have you said anything? Do they suspect anything? They will kill me.'

'Don't be stupid. I'm not going to say anything. I don't think they have guessed… yes, they will… your mum has always said not to rush these things. I think she will be disappointed in me.'

I stood there in shock at what I had hoped I hadn't heard, but now I had. How was I going to handle this all at once? I wanted to go and slap him. He had taken my little girl away. She had taken a huge step in the adult world. 'Get a grip, Alice. You know it would happen some day. Just pretend you heard nothing. She may want to talk to you, and you have to be understanding and slapping him will not help,' I was talking to myself.

'Hello, Alice. Where's Martin?' Simon was looking at me.

I stood there just looking at the pair of them. I was being pathetic, or was I just being a mum? 'Oh sorry, I was miles away. He's in the kitchen.'

There was no way I was going to tell Martin, not until I knew from Kerry. I was sure she would talk to me sooner or later.

Monday morning and I was up early getting ready for work thinking about Kerry. My nerves were so bad I couldn't eat. Normally with the worry of Kerry I would be eating anything going. Everyone was up eating whatever they wanted. The kids ready for school. I looked at Kerry in her uniform. She looked like my little girl again, but she was leaving school in three weeks. I had to face facts she was not a little girl, but she still has a lot to learn.

'I'm going now,' I called.

'Good luck, love.' Martin gave me a kiss goodbye.

'Don't burn the chickens.' Sandra and Daisy laughed.

'What time do you finish?' asked Kerry.

'About five, why?'

'No reason, have fun,' and she went upstairs.

Abbey was waiting for me. I was grateful for that. She showed me around where to put my things and told me who was who and what they did and so on.

I was shown how to cook the chickens. How to make sure they were hot enough and cooked properly. Before I knew it Abbey was calling me for break time.

We went to the café. It was busy but then it always is. The coffee was a bit weak, but the chocolate cake was yummy, moist and light with chocolate pieces in it. Back to work and the cake was killing me. Thankfully, Abbey was an expert with the café, so she knew we would need something for our indigestion.

Time to serve my first customer. I was shaking like a leaf. A nice little elderly lady came to me. She was all clean and cute (you know what I mean). I handed her what she had asked for. 'Are you alright, dear?' she asked.

'She is fine. It's her first day,' Abbey explained.

'Oh, I would have thought a lady of your age would be over all that, but I suppose when you get to a certain age you have to be more careful if you lose your job. It's less likely you will get another. Well, goodbye, dear.'

'Well, there I was thinking what a nice little old lady to serve, and it turns out she's an old bat.'

'Come on... ' Abbey was laughing.

Abbey showed me how to clean down the spit roasts and the trays, and what cleaner to use on what. I never knew there was so much to it.

'Are you two not going for lunch?' Lizzie asked. Lizzie is a hardworking girl. It appears she is never late, and everyone likes her. Today she is in charge.

'What? Oh, look at the time. Now wonder I'm hungry.' Abbey was on her way for food.

I would have liked to say that we walked to the café, but Abbey was hungry so we were nearing a sprint to the café. I settled for a sandwich, fruit cocktail and water. When I got my breath back I started my lunch.

'Is that all you're having?' Abbey looked horrified.

'Yes, that's all I want. I have been bad already, and all my hard work will go out the window if I'm not careful. I munched my lunch as Abbey tucked into what looked like half the food in the café.

I was glad I only had a sandwich, as after lunch we had a delivery. So there was a lot of lifting to do and checking that everything was there. At about four we went to tea break. I was glad of that. I needed a cuppa and a small chocolate bar. I think I needed it for the energy more than anything.

After tea break Abbey was to show me the pizza counter. How much topping to put on and so on. I thought, at one point during the day that my brain was going to go bang with all the things I had to remember.

There was cheese, onion, pepperoni, pineapple… you name it, and it was there. 'Abbey can you show Alice where we keep the fresh topping, please?' The lady in charge of the pizza counter asked.

We went out to the back where a huge fridge stood. It had lots of shelves full up with things that we needed for the pizza. She showed me how to rotate the stock, and how to make sure I marked down everything I took from the fridge, so that we will know at a glance what we will need to order, and how quickly the stock can go mainly at weekends.

Suddenly it was time to go home. I had forgotten all about my problems at home, until I got in the car and they all came flooding back. What to do about Kerry and Simon? Do I tell Martin? Who was going to be with the kids in the holidays? Did Martin still have a job? My head was spinning with all the new things to remember and now all the problems trying to squeeze in as well.

I stopped for petrol on the way home and had a sugar fix. It always helps when I'm worried.

I got home to all the questions about my day, 'don't wait for me at dinner. I'm not in.'

'You still going to the gym after your first day at work?' Martin sounded surprised.

'I have to. We eat in the café everyday and do they do some nice things in there.'

Pat picked me up at about seven that evening. She was not her normal self. She was fed up, 'I don't want to go to the gym,' she told me.

'OK, where shall we go?' If she didn't want to go to the gym then who was I to argue?

'There is a nice little pub just down from the gym, fancy that?'

'Fine by me.'

We pulled into the pub car park. It was very quiet and a bit spooky. We walked quickly across to the door and went in like we were brave about anything. We ordered a drink and sat down. We had a good choice of seats seeing as we were the only ones in there.

'Fancy something to eat?' I asked her.

'I was going to ask you that,' she sounded better already.

We scanned the menu, taking our time. 'There's chicken curry,' I said.

'We can't have that. We will stink of curry when we go home. Then they will know.'

'I didn't think of that. What a shame. OK, I will have… pie and chips.'

'That sounds good. Then I'm going to have the jam steamed pudding and custard.'

'That does sound yummy.' We ordered two pie and chips and two jam puddings and another drink, only cola so no one will know.

The chips were big, fat ones (no, not to match the person eating them, thank you). The pie was full of huge chunks of beef in rich gravy. The pastry was puffy and golden and crumbly. We ate every little bit. The pudding was as good. The custard was thick and creamy. The pudding was light and spongy with a good amount of jam on top. We washed it all down with another cola.

'This is much better than the gym,' I said.

'You bet. We will have to do this again.'

Pat's children are older than mine; so I asked her advise about Kerry. It was good to talk to someone about it. She was very helpful. We chatted for ages, it was a good sister's night out.

'You're late,' Martin said as I walked in the door.

'It was very busy, we had to keep waiting for the machines to be free.'

'Do you want a cup of tea and something to eat?'

'Just a cup of tea, please. It's a bit late to eat.'

'OK, I will do it while you take a shower.'

I went to bed feeling very full up and happy.

Tuesday and I was up and looking forward to my day at work. I was lucky all the people that I worked with seemed to be very nice and helpful.

The week was gone before I knew what was happening. 'I have to work late on Fridays. I'm sorry, Sandra darling.'

'How late do you have to work?'

'I don't finish until eleven at night.'

'Don't worry, Sandra love. We can go bowling if you want.' Martin gave her a hug.

'Yeah, thanks, Dad. That will be great. Can we have fried chicken as well?'

'Well, I don't know about that. You're pushing it a bit.' He smiled.

'That's nice bowling and fried chicken without me,' I said.

'Never mind, Mum. It will help your diet.'

Diet… I must have tried every cake in the café. We all sang 'Happy Birthday' to Sandra as she opened her presents. Her best was from Kerry. It was her very own box of chocolates. I made her favourite breakfast that was pancakes with maple syrup. We all had some. They were very nice.

I decorated the house for Sandra before I went to work and then I had lunch. All the milkshakes were gone, so I couldn't have them. I know what I really fancy, I put the oil in a pan to heat up and then I spread two pieces of bread. The oil was hot, so I put in a good handful of chips. It's amazing how many you can get in your hand when need be. When they were cooked, I made my sandwich. I never wasted time on cutting it, just took a huge bite.

'I suppose that sandwich is going to have to last you until tonight, is it?' Martin was home for lunch.

'Well, you are going for fried chicken.'

'You're not doing well on your diet at the moment, are you?'

'No, not really. Does it show that much?'

'Yes, it does. You're putting on all the weight you lost, again.'

'I know. I'm finding it really hard. We eat at the café everyday.'

'Why don't you just give up?'

'No, I will try harder, and I will do better at the gym.'

'You would do better, if you went to the gym.' He was laughing.

'What do you mean? I do go to the gym.' I had a feeling I had been found out.

' Monday, you did not eat as it was too late, or was it more like because you and Pat had eaten in the pub? You know John, I work with? He saw you.'

'Well, we needed to talk. Pat was feeling down, and I didn't want to tell you in case you got cross.'

I finished my lunch and set off for work. It was a long night and very slow.   Not many people in, and I was thinking about Sandra and if she was having a good birthday. Finally, time to go home.

'Mum, you're home,' Sandra told me all about her day.

'Hi, love, want a cuppa? What's in the bag? You look worn out,' Martin was talking at me.

'Chicken and barbecue ribs. Every Friday and Saturday we can buy what is left for silly prices.'

I couldn't face any fried chicken that they had left. I had eaten at the café with Abbey. We had chicken curry and because it was late, the girl had piled my plate up. I couldn't eat it all. It was a shame, as it was so nice, but I was so full that I even had to save my chocolate bar for later.

Saturday, and I don't start work until four this afternoon. I got on the scales and instantly wished I hadn't. It flashed 81 kilograms. I could have cried.

Martin and the girls went shopping while I did the housework and got ready for work. Now I will need lunch before work. I looked in all the cupboards, but there was nothing. I know I fancy a burger, so off I went.

I sat down with my large meal and was enjoying it very much until…

'I can see you are trying harder on your diet,' Martin was looking down at me.

'What are you doing in here? You never said you were coming here,' I was so shocked.

'What am I doing? Well, I like that, and you never said you were coming in here either.'

'I didn't see you. Where are the girls? If I had seen you, I would have sat with you.'

'They are just getting their lunch before we go home. Feeling a bit peckish, are we?' He was looking at my food. I was feeling guilty.

He had nothing, the girls were getting theirs and I was stuffing my face.

'Hello, Mum. What you doing in here? There you go, Dad... your big Mac, large fries, large cola and a bacon burger. We got it right, didn't we?'

'Well, answer Sandra dear. You pig, you are to have all that, and you were looking like you weren't going to have anything. I should have known.' I laughed.

'Well, I'm trying hard on my diet... like you,' he grinned.

We all sat together and ate our food and laughed about it all. Then I went to work and my family went home. I watched them go. Although I love my job, I still deep down that I was going home with them. I got in the car and went to work.

We were very busy all afternoon. I don't think I had ever seen so many people in one place before, it was mad. At about half past seven I looked up from checking the chickens to see a face I knew coming towards me. It was Sharon.

'Oh hello, I didn't know you worked here, but I suppose it's as good a place as any if you have to work,' she smirked.

'This is Elizabeth. Elizabeth, this is Alice, the one I told you about,' said Sharon.

'Pleased, I'm sure. We don't normally come into the lower class of supermarket, but we are in a hurry,' snooty Elizabeth told me.

'Really? Well, what do you want?' I know it's my job, but I was finding it hard being nice.

'I will have the plumpest and juiciest barbeque chicken that you have in the shop.' Elizabeth glared at me.

'We don't want too much sauce. We like our food delicately flavoured,' Sharon put in.

'I will see what we have out the back. Won't keep you long, a moment,' I put on the poshest voice I could.

Lizzie was bagging up some hot chicken and had a lovely one in her hand, 'I will do that for you, it's your tea break.' I smiled.

I took the chicken from her and looked for a cloth to wipe the sauce off with. There was not one to be found, so I compromised. Using my finger I wiped all the sauce off. The bit that my finger couldn't reach, I used my tongue and the sauce was good. The only problem was that I had a cold coming. I found some new sauce in a pot. It looked the nicest, so I put some on the chicken and bagged it up.

I was feeling a bit bad about what I had just done until I got to the counter, and I could hear the horrible things they were saying about me. They looked startled as I approached, 'the best in the shop. Any problems just bring it back.' I smiled sweetly.

'We would rather throw it way than come in here again,' I reckoned that's what they would say.

At break I told Abbey what I had done. 'What sauce was it?' she asked.

'The one in the green pot.'

'We are not allowed to use that; you will be in such trouble if anyone finds out.' She looked worried.

'Why it looked fine.'

'That's the extra hot, green chilli sauce. Someone made it, but it was so hot no one could eat it.'

'Good, that will sort the old cow out.'

When I got home at about half past midnight, I found Martin asleep in the armchair. I made a cup of tea and sat down. Martin sort of opened an eye at me. We tucked into the chicken and ribs I had got, and I told him all about the chicken and why I had done it. He said he would have done the same. I put all the cakes and bread, which I had got very cheap, away and went to bed.

Sunday and no work. I'm not getting up until ten o'clock. I don't know why, I'm just not. When I did get up, I found Sandra and Daisy tucking into their breakfast.

'That's not a very good breakfast. Couldn't you find anything better?'

'Yeah, but we wanted this and dad said it was OK,' they both said at once.

'That's good of him. Now move over and pass the cakes about.' I smiled.

'You're not allowed,' protested Daisy.

'Says who?' I asked as I stuffed a whole chocolate cake in my mouth.

'What are you doing? You're a bad influence on them girls.' Martin had come in from the garden.

'What I found them eating then, they said you let them have it.'

'Yes, I let them but not you. Now pass them around.' He sat with us. We managed to eat our way through three packets of cakes and a packet of chocolate wafers.

I suddenly realized I was a child short, 'Where's Kerry?'

'She went babysitting for one of Simon's mum's friend. They were going to be late so she stayed at Simon's,' Martin explained.

'That's fine,' I tried to keep my voice normal, but Martin picked up on it.

'What's the matter? Don't you like her staying at Simon's? Don't worry she is a sensible girl, she must be... she takes after me,' he beamed.

'That's what worries me.' I laughed.

I was lucky Martin had got all the school things ready, so all I had to do was a bit of tidying up and cook dinner.

In the afternoon I fancied something nice to eat, but I just didn't know what, so I thought for a moment. I knew if I nibbled a little of everything then I should be OK. I got all the different sorts of cakes out of the cupboard and cut a little slice of the end of each and put them on a plate. Then I found whatever chocolate I could and had a piece off each. Next I looked in the fridge. Do I fancy something savoury or not? I still didn't know, so I added some cheese and a small bit of pork pie, then a few crackers. 'There that should sort out what I fancy.' I put myself and my plate of goodies in front of the telly. Everyone else was doing whatever, so I had the front room to myself.

I ate my way through my goodies, but still I felt that I fancied something else. A cheese-toasted sandwich smelt great, the only problem with food like that is that it attracts the others, and in no time the family were eating toasted cheese sandwiches. Kerry and Simon came in about 6 o'clock, so the house was full again.

'Have I missed dinner, Mum?' Kerry called from the kitchen cupboard.

'No, it will be about another hour yet.'

'Mum, what's happened to the cakes? It looks like someone has cut the ends of them all.'

I was thinking as fast as I could, 'Oh no! Who would have done that? I will ask the others later. We did have some for breakfast, but they really must not do this sort of thing.' I hope I was convincing enough.

'I will ask now if you want. Can we have some?'

'No, it's OK. I will sort it. Thank you and yes, you can have some.' I hope she doesn't say anything.

'Can Simon stay for dinner? His mum has gone out,' she asked with a mouthful of cake.

'Yes, where's she gone? Somewhere nice?' I asked.

'She has a boyfriend, and he has taken her away for the weekend. She needed a break.'

'So you stayed at Simon's without his mum there?'

There was a long pause. 'His sister was there.'

'Where do you sleep when you stay?' I asked.

Martin was looking at me and then at Simon. I knew what he was thinking, and I think Simon had guessed. He went into the kitchen very quickly. We could hear them whispering.

'You two alright out there?' Martin called.

'Yes, fine.'

Kerry and Simon brought the coffee into the front room. Martin looked at them and grinned, 'we are not stupid, you know. We know what you two have been up to, telling us you sleep in his sister's room. Now let's see if I get this right: no one at home, so order a pizza, maybe, and a bottle of something, seeing as the house is all yours for the night. Then Bob's your uncle, so to speak.'

Kerry and Simon looked like they would die of embarrassment. I was a little shocked myself, he seemed so calm. I needed chocolate, so I took myself off to the kitchen to start dinner and found a little lonely chocolate cake in the cupboard. I felt sorry for it being all alone, so I ate it.

Dinner was a little tense to say the least, but we got through it. At last it was time for Simon to go home. After he had gone Kerry came to talk to me, 'I'm sorry I lied about sleeping in Simon's sister's room. I just didn't want you to think bad of me.'

'How can I feel bad about you? It's life, just be careful and hope that he is not using you or you using him. It works both ways.'

'No, we are not really, I was thinking of going to the doctor's to talk to him about precautions.' She looked a bit embarrassed.

'That's a sensible thing to do, but you know that I will have to go with you. You are only fifteen. There is nothing I can do about it. That's the rules, OK?'

'I know, thanks mum, good night.'

That was not a conversation that I wanted with my fifteen year old but there we go, I've had it. I lay awake for hours thinking about the day and how my life has turned out and how fast the kids are growing up. It was a good job. I didn't have any chocolates left in my draw.

Chapter Nine

Monday and off we go again. Kerry was getting ready for her last week at school. 'That's it. She can look after the other two and do some housework for me, and I can pay her.' I told myself, as I got ready for work. Not that I wanted to go today, I was feeling tired.

We seemed to be extra busy on the pizza counter today, and we needed things from the fridge, but Abbey didn't like going to the fridge in case the door closes on her. 'OK, I'll go,' I said, and off I plodded. The fridge always smelt good, but today it smelt really good with the cheeses, the hams and the onions that all smelt so fresh. It took me a while to find everything as I was still unsure where it all was. Then suddenly a piece of ham jumped from my hand and into my mouth. I don't know how it happened, but I'm glad it did. If I got caught, then I would be sacked.

'You were gone for long.' Abbey grinned.

'I was trying to find it all.'

We needed a lot more from the fridge, so I offered to go each time. The cheese was creamy and strong, and the ham was juicy and sweet. I was careful not to have the onion or anything smelly, and so I had a good morning picking.

Abbey and I went to tea break to find that the café people were doing sausages in French bread with fried onions. The smell was great, but the only problem was do I have the normal or the jumbo size. I looked at them. Both the sausage was fat and juicy with herbs in it. The onions were crisp, the bread was golden. Abbey and I looked at each other, and then we looked at the lady waiting to serve us. 'Jumbo sausage, please,' we said at the same time.

Alison Woodward

We finished our lovely sausages, and we had finally finished giggling about the sausages. You would have thought that ladies of our age would know how to behave, but Abbey had said something unmentionable about our food and that was it. We were off. I was told that I would be on the chicken counter, which was a good thing. That meant I didn't have to go to the fridge and face all the lovely tempting things in there that jump out at me.

The chicken counter was very busy, so maybe I might have lost some of the fat that I had gained eating the sausages, but I doubt it. Fat just clings to me, it's not fussy. Often you hear other people saying that fat goes on the hips or legs or whatever, not my fat because it just goes wherever it finds a space. At the moment I am short on space, so no doubt it is just sitting on top of some other lump.

I tried to be good for lunch. I had just a salad and a bottle of water. I don't know who I'm trying to kid. A salad is not going to do a lot when I've already had a half-pound of lard for a snack. What planet am I on today?

At last I'm on my way home, and I managed not to eat anything all afternoon. I'm sure that will help until I'm really hungry. I eat enough for two, but not tonight. I'm off to the gym, I think or maybe the pub… that would be good. Now, come on Alice, get motivated… stop thinking of food and drink. In the door at last, and just in time for a cuppa, then change for the gym.

'I'm just making you a cuppa, and Pat had called. She said she couldn't make it tonight. She has a cold,' Martin called from the kitchen. I was a little disappointed about it. The evening got worse, Martin burnt the veg curry. 'Don't ask how I just couldn't tell you… Simon came round to say that he has lost his job due to someone stealing, and seeing as his past is a bit dark they blamed him,' he said. I was fed up and we all know what happens when I'm fed up. 'I'm making coffee. Anyone want one?' Everybody wanted coffee, so twenty minutes later I came in with coffee and a huge chocolate cake. It even had grated chocolate on top. Though it was thick, gooey and sickly it was still very good. It was even better when we poured fresh double cream all over it.

The week just went from bad to worse. Tuesday Sandra broke her leg, Wednesday Daisy and her best friend had a fall out, so she was upset. Thursday our rabbit died and Friday Martin lost his job, and God, did I eat a lot of chocolate in that week? However, by Friday I was fed up. I also had a big bag of sweets and a bottle of wine. If I'm not diabetic by next week then I just don't know.

Saturday and I'm not even going to think about weighing myself. I know I'm bigger now than when I started this the so-called diet months ago. I'm so useless. 'Now come on, Alice, don't get down. Just get ready for work.' You know I thought that when I started work again, I would stop talking to myself, but I think I'm doing it more.

We were so busy at work that I missed my tea break, but it didn't bother me. It still bothered me that I was not worried about missing tea break because that meant no food. 'Am I falling ill? No, just get on with your job. I'm doing it again, talking to myself.' By lunch I was starving. It's not good, but I wanted a salad and fruit for pudding. I had a nice cheese salad and a kiwi fruit for after. It was quiet as Abbey was on the late shift, and I would be going home when she comes in. I felt odd without her. I missed her daft jokes, but I'm sure I will survive.

We were busy all day. There was no let up at all. By about three o'clock I was feeling worn out, and I would be glad for four o'clock when I finish. 'Alice you missed your tea break this morning. I know you only an hour to go, but go and get a drink. You can have 15 minutes.' My supervisor was a fair lady. She never let you do more than you should, and I was glad at that moment. I dragged myself off to the café. I was gasping for a drink.

I plonked myself on a chair with a bottle of water and a fruit trifle. I know it's not for diets but I fancied it. It is nice to have a bit of what you fancy sometimes. I heard a voice that I recognized as moaning. I looked round to find Sharon moaning away to a lady I didn't know, 'Can you believe it, she went without me after all the things I've done for her, and she promised I could go. She is as bad as that Alice I was friends with. Don't know why I was friends with her. She is so fat and has nothing to offer. She really cramped my style… ' Sharon was going on and on about Elizabeth and me. At first I was getting upset, then anger set in. I had had enough. I walked over to her, she looked shocked, 'You are a bitter old cow,'

I said as I plonked my trifle on her head, 'wash it down with this,' I told her and I tipped the bottle of whatever all over her. I didn't care who was watching. I glanced over my shoulder as I walked away and saw Sharon just sitting there dripping with trifle and water. She looked a mess with her make up all down her face. I grinned all the way back to work.

About 20 minutes later I was called to the office. Sharon had put in a complaint about me. I explained to my supervisor what had happened and what had been said. She found it funny that I had put trifle on someone's head and she understood why, but she had to give me a warning. That's fair enough, it's her job. I'm lucky I suppose, I could have lost mine.

I got home to find everyone as fed up as I had been feeling. 'Lets get out of here,' I suggested

'Yeah, where? Asked Sandra.

'The cinema, then the pizza place.'

'OK, but what's on? Why are men never any help?'

'I don't know. Let's just go and look, and if there is nothing then we will just eat.' I snapped.

There were too many of us to fit in our car, so Simon followed us on his scooter. We took a while looking at the board on the cinema wall and decided that there was nothing that any of us wanted to see. So what to do now? Martin came up with the idea of going bowling. He does like that, and so off we went. The bowling alley was just a few yards from the cinema, so that was handy and the pizza place was just next-door. So I didn't have to waddle around too much.

The bowling was great fun, and it made us all feel better. I was ready for my pizza but then that's nothing unusual for me. I'm always ready for food. We walked along to the pizza place, and I caught a glimpse of myself in a window I was horrified. I was waddling like a duck. I felt ashamed of myself, and I felt angry that I had let myself become something like this, so I promised myself that Monday on I will diet properly. This time I had a gut feeling that I was going to do it right, but this evening I was going to enjoy myself.

We sat at a large, round table looking at the menu while the waiter got us a drink, and then asked if we were ready to order. By the time he had asked for the fourth time I could tell he was getting fed up. Simon suggested that we have a selection of different pizzas, so we could all try them. So the waiter went away happy at last. We left the pizza place about half past ten. Kerry went to stay at Simon's. I was not happy about it, but if I say no she will only lie to me to get to stay, so they went on his scooter and off we went home.

I was up first and was enjoying a quiet cup of tea, 'What can I have for breakfast?' I asked myself. I could have a bowl of fresh fruit chopped up. I just fancy that.

'Morning, Mum… Oh no, you're not going to make us eat all that diet stuff again?' Sandra was looking in my bowl.

'No, I just fancied this, but I am going to try harder.'

'Whatever.' She looked at me on her way to the kitchen. I can't understand why they have no faith in me.

'Tell your dad I've gone for a bike ride when he gets up, please,' I told Sandra.

'OK, I'll get a nice, soft cushion for you when you get back,' she laughed.

'Ha, ha… very funny.'

It was about two hours later that I got home. My bum was numb, my legs didn't want to go, but I walked as normal as possible to make it look good. I got inside and fell on to the sofa. I wouldn't have minded if I had gone a long way, but I had only done about half an hour of peddling when I met Abbey. She was out for a walk, so I had spent the rest of the time talking, but I'm not telling this lot. I decided to get a bath to soothe the pains.

Getting up the stairs was like climbing the tallest mountain, and I'm sure someone had moved the bathroom a mile away from where it used to be. Even the taps seemed to have been turned off very tightly. At last I slid into the warm water with bubbles everywhere. It was heaven. I must have dropped off, as the next thing I knew Martin was knocking on the door to tell me that he had made coffee.

Good, I thought. I can have some biscuits as well, but first I had to get out. The warm water had help my aching legs and getting out was easier than I thought it would have been, 'That's not so bad,' I told myself as I went into the kitchen.

We had coffee and I chose chocolate biscuits. I needed the chocolate for energy, you understand. I had used a lot up this morning, and I needed to replace it. So I ate half the packet. I was good; I could have eaten all the packet... I wanted to really, but Martin wouldn't let me. He's so boring.

Monday and the alarm was ringing in my ear. I turned over and put out a hand to turn it off. The pain shot up my arm. I must have reach out wrong, I thought. I put my legs out of bed to get up, but the pain was worse than in my arms, 'Oh, my legs,' I yelled. I had forgotten that it's the next day when the pain sets in. I got up, but I don't know how.

'You OK?' Martin was laughing.

'No, I think I might have to ring in sick. I hurt so much,' I grumped.

I went to work praying that we wouldn't be too busy. I also had to look normal, as Abbey knew that I had not been far on the bike, and I will never live it down if she sees me suffering. So off I went in to work, trying so hard not to walk like a chocolate soldier.

I did my best all day, and lucky for me we were not very busy. My limbs were loosening up by the end of my shift. I had been very good with my diet. I just knew I had to try. I had a sandwich all day, but at every break time the chocolates were shouting out to me. The cakes were calling my name, even the golden syrup on the sponge pudding had grown arms and was trying to pull me to them, but today I was the strongest. I don't know about tomorrow, but today I won.

Home, at last, and I could flop down. Oh no, dinner to sort out first, even though Martin was at home he never seemed to have enough time to sort out dinner. I would love to know what he does all day. Maybe, I should spy on him one day.

I got in to find Martin waiting with a cup of tea and the dinner all prepared. I looked at him grinning at me. 'He wants something.' I thought. 'Well, he's out of luck. I'm knackered.'

'Don't look at me like that; I don't want anything,' he said.

'Well, now I'm even more worried.' I thought.

'Well, when I say I don't want any thing, that's not quite what I meant. I want to ask you something, it's something I've been thinking about a lot, and I want to know how you would feel about it. You don't have to rush, I will give you time.' He was still grinning stupidly.

I was getting increasingly worried. To my knowledge there is only one thing most men think about a lot. So what's he been up to, maybe I am going to find out why he never has time to do the dinner. 'Just get on with it and stop babbling.' I was also getting inpatient.

'OK, how do you feel about moving?' He grinned.

'Is that it? Is that all you wanted to know? Well, where do you have in mind?' He often comes up with the moving thing then changes his mind.

'How about France, we all loved it.'

'What do the kids think? You know holidaying there and living there are two very different things.' He had taken me aback by saying France.

'I haven't said anything to the kids. I wanted to know what you would think.'

'I don't think Kerry will go. She and Simon are very close.' My brain was hurting more than my body now, all this and I haven't even finished my drink or barely got my coat off.

'I was thinking about that too.'

'Oh lord, help us.'

'Don't be like that. We could ask if he wants to come with us. He has no job, and things might be better for him there, what do you think?'

'I think you have gone mad sitting here all day, but if you are serious then we can talk to the kids tonight when I get back from the gym. I'm going to get ready now.'

Pat and I pulled up outside the gym. None of us were very eager to go in. Pat looked at me, 'What's the matter?'

' Martin wants us to move to France,' I told her as we got out the car and made our way to the door.

'And you're not too sure.' She smiled. 'I don't feel like doing this tonight.'

'No, I'm not sure what to do. I can't speak French.' I sighed as we got back in the car.

We settled ourselves in a corner of the chip shop and Pat told me that I should go for it. She said she would miss us all, but what have we got here. Martin was out of work, Kerry leaving school in a few days and no job. She got me thinking. Maybe she was right. It's a shame I was not thinking as hard about what I was eating as I was about moving. We had cod and chips with onion rings and a Cola each.

'Why is it whenever I have fish and chips I always want something sweet after?' Pat was asking me.

'I don't know. It's odd, but I don't have to eat fish and chips to want something sweet.' We laughed as we pulled up outside the off-license. We both had a chocolate bar and a bottle of Bacardi drink thing with cola in it. We sat in the car eating drinking and chatting.

It had been raining all evening, so I was glad that it had stopped by the time Pat dropped me off a few houses down from mine. As I walked along, I realized that I didn't even look like I had been to the gym, and Martin was sure to notice. I had to think fast. I put my towel round my neck in hope that that would help, but it did nothing really. So I had another idea, I found a large puddle and splashed water on my hair, under my arms, around my bust to make it look like I had worked really hard. Then I rubbed my hair a bit with the towel for a good effect, and then I checked myself as best I could in the puddle. When I felt I looked right I walked in through the gate. I had a fright as two pairs of eyes were looking at me. Kerry was saying goodnight to Simon and had seen everything I had done. I looked at them out the corner of my eye as I passed, 'Don't ask.'

'You're late, and you look worn out and sweaty. You get a shower, and I will get you something to eat and drink.' Martin was being extra kind.

'Thanks, but it's too late to eat. We are late because we worked extra hard. We did longer on everything,' I lied. If I keep these lies going this way, I will never go to heaven when my time comes, I told myself as I showered.

Downstairs Martin was waiting with a cup of tea, 'Are the kids in bed?' I asked

'Yes, they were tired. Have you thought any more about moving?'

'I did talk to Pat about it and says we should go for it, but we do need to talk to the kids. We will have to do that tomorrow as they are in bed now.'

'OK, and you're tired from the gym,' he smiled.

'Yeah, I'm about ready for my bed.' I faked a yawn, and went off to bed.

Tuesday and my day off, but I was still up at half past seven and so was everyone else. Kerry looked at me. 'Morning, Mum... bet you ache all over after you worked so hard at the gym. You were very sweaty,' she said with a cheeky grin.

'No, I'm fine. Thank you.' I gave her a look that said – you say anything and you're in trouble.

'I think it would do dad good to go to the gym with you. It would get him out of here.'

'There is no room for him. I have asked.'

'I finish school at lunchtime, and dad said he would pick me up seeing as he is going to town.'

'OK, I will get you some lunch. Have a good day.' I couldn't believe that she leaves school next week and then to only have half a day today.

While I was on my own, I got on with the ironing. It helps to keep my mind off food. I had just finished and was putting the kettle on when the doorbell went.

'Hi Abbey, what brings you here?'

'I saw Martin in town, and he said you were in and that it would be OK for me to pop in. Hope you don't mind.'

'No, it's good to see you. I was making tea, come in.'

We sat down with our tea and Abbey opened a little white box that she had with her. As I told her about us thinking about moving to France, she handed me a huge gypsy tart and one for herself. I looked at her, ' Well, Martin said he would be a couple of hours, so I thought we needed something to fill the time.' She smiled.

We both took a huge bite and both had cake round our faces. We were like big kids, so we decided that we were not allowed to lick our lips until we were finished. We were in such a mess, but it was great fun.

'You can only go to France, if I can visit you lots,' she said with gypsy tart stuck to her nose.

'You can come to see us when you want.'

We were so busy chatting that we didn't realize what the time was. Suddenly the front door opened and Martin and Kerry came in. It was a good job that we had got rid of the box and little foil dishes that the cakes came in.

'Hope you are hungry. We thought you might be with all the talking you two can do, so we brought lunch in with us,' Martin was saying as he came in with a bargain box of fried chicken, chips and a bottle of Cola.

'Oh, thank you. We are starving.' Abbey was smiling, I though I could eat but abbey takes some beating.

We all chattered on about moving. Kerry was keen to go but didn't want to leave Simon, so we explained what Martin had suggested. She said she would talk to him and his mum tonight.

On the way home we stopped off at your gym, and they said that dad could join whenever he wanted to. That's good news, don't you think?'

' Err… yeah, that's great. I'll call Pat tonight. I'm sure she will be as thrilled as I am.' Thrilled… I could have murdered her. Pat and I had planed to go to the pizza place next week, and now they have spoilt it all.

Abbey went home and Martin went in search for a new home in France. I don't know why he was looking; we haven't even had our house valued yet. He has no idea what it's worth, but if I say anything he will say he knows about how much houses are worth, and we still haven't spoken to the girls about it yet. God, do I need chocolate?

When the girls came in, we all talked about moving. They seemed OK about it. They wanted a big leaving party for all their friends and family. They were still on about what kind of house they would like when I was dishing up their dinner. All through dinner they chatted about the move. I was glad I wasn't eating. All the talking would have given me indigestion. At last it was time for them to go to bed. Martin and I spent a couple of hours on the Internet looking and printing out houses that the girls might like.

Chapter Ten

Wednesday and the alarm was going mad in my ear, and I was starving. I made a fruit cocktail for breakfast. I thought it might help as my clothes were growing every time. I got dressed. The fruit was nice but not very filling, but I will just have to put up with it. I just don't know what else to do other than locking myself in a dungeon for a few months… now, that's a good idea. We agreed with Kerry to talk to Simon tonight about moving because she said he went quiet when she told him, and his mum thought he would love to come with us if we let him.

At last, I was at work. It was a lot quieter here than at home. I found Abbey waiting for me with a cup of tea. 'Morning, you look knackered. I'm joining a slimming club. It's the only way for me to lose weight, want to come?' she asked all hopeful.

'Where, when and how much?'

' OK, Monday evenings. Next road to mine and I don't know.'

'I go to the gym on Mondays, but I will ask Pat if we can change nights.'

'That would be great. I don't want to go on my own. I'm sure we will have fun.'

'We only have a few days to pig out, so I'm going to enjoy them.' Abbey had a wicked smile on her and knew what that meant.

By tea break I was starving (I know you don't have to tell me). So Abbey and I went to the café. It was so hard trying to decide what I wanted, really, I wanted one of everything, but that would have been more than pigging out. So I settled for the biggest breakfast that they do. It was good, and not greasy at all. Even the fried bread was good, just crisp with no fat. After we were full we made our way back to work, but got distracted by a new chocolate that was looking at us saying 'Try me.'

'Wow, look at that, Abbey, a new low fat chocolate bar called Free Yourself, and it only has 60 calories a bar. Do you think we would be allowed to try them on the slimming club diet?'

'What? I don't care, I'm having one now. What flavours are there? Yes, minty one... ' And off she went to pay for it. 'You not having one?' she asked.

'No, I'm so full up, maybe later.... No, Abbey, I'm not ill, so don't look at me like that.'

After break I just wanted to go home. Everything I did went wrong. I lost count how many chickens I had dropped. The ones without sauce were OK. I just dusted them off. No one will know and seeing as I was on my own that made it easier, but the ones with sauce I had to bin. I did think about washing them but then I thought better of it. To make things worse we started to get busy. I was late to lunch as Tina and Lizzie were not back from their lunch and it was two o'clock. My tummy felt like it was six o'clock. How I wished I had got some of those chocolate bars. I could have sneaked one or two.

Tina and Lizzie arrived back at half past two, so Abbey, who by then was helping me, set off for lunch. I don't know why I was bothering as I only had a few hours until I went home, but if I eat now then Martin can cook for himself and the girls. I can go on the Internet to look for houses.

Abbey and I had the chicken curry. It was hot, nice but hot. We were enjoying it when a voice that we knew echoed around us, 'You're having your lunch late.' We looked round to find Martin smiling at us.

'What are doing here?' I asked.

'Well, my little chicken, I have been to the estate agents, and they said that we won't have a problem selling our type of house.' He was looking all-smug.

'That's good, but I'm still unsure about going. I can't speak French and trying to get the kids in school will be a nightmare.'

'It's a new start for us all. I will get a job. I will do anything, I don't mind.' He was dead keen to go.

'We will talk when I get in, I have to go now.'

I was half glad to be going home, but then again I will have to talk houses again. I need a nice bath I decided, so when I got in I told Martin we will talk later and that he was cooking tonight and I was going for a bath.

Martin, Kerry, Sandra and Daisy spent ages on the Internet looking at houses. They all agreed on a nice house with 3 acres of land and a large outbuilding that was not attached to the house. This, they decided, Simon could have so that he could turn it into his own place. Then if he and Kerry split up, he will still have somewhere to live, and seeing as he will pay us rent there won't be a problem. Kerry called him up to tell him.

I stood there listening and watching, feeling like I don't matter. I'm not here. Don't count me in. I made myself a cup of tea and headed for the garden saying on my way 'Am I on any of your plans, or do I just do as I'm told. After all I must be the child here, so therefore I don't need consulting.'.

I felt pressured into doing something I was unsure about. I had had my home chosen for me, even who was going to live there and what they were going to do with it. They didn't need me, nor were they going to listen to me. I felt sad. I had two choices, I give in and go, or I lose my family as I felt sure they would go without me and I didn't, at the end of the day, want to lose my family.

I went back into the lounge where they were all chattering. Even Simon had come round; Martin gave me the paperwork on the house. It looked a very nice house. It was big and only a fraction of the price we had paid for this house seven years ago. They were all looking at me, 'What do you think?' Martin asked.

'Does it matter what I think? You will need to see it.' I was still agitated as I pulled a Free Yourself bar from my bag. I don't think I would have cared if it was the most fattening bar in the world, at that moment I needed chocolate.

'You are not supposed to be eating chocolate,' Daisy said wagging her finger at me.

'So now you think you can tell me what to eat as well as choose my home.' She had not chosen a good time.

'Don't be like that, love. I thought you wanted us all to like the new house.' Martin was looking pathetic.

'Yes, I wanted us all to like the new house, but seeing as I don't get a look in, what does it matter?' and I stomped out.

'If it's a really nice house, do you want me to put an offer in?'

Men… why are they so insensitive? They don't know when to stop. 'Do what you want,' and I poured myself a large glass of wine.

I was trying to feel the same as the rest of them, but it just wouldn't come, so I took myself into the garden again with my wine and three bars of chocolate. It would have been better to have had some dinner, but you know me.

Thursday and I was feeling a bit better. I had to start at eight o'clock this morning, so I was leaving Martin to see to the kids and I was gone before everyone was up.

I met Abbey in the café for coffee and toast. They do that for the early shift. Abbey was in a silly mood today, and that cheered me up no end.

Our supervisor was a grumpy old lady today, and she had told us off for acting younger than our years. We were only throwing pizza base boards at each other to put the pizzas on. OK, we got confused sometimes and throw pizza bases instead, but we caught them and there was nothing on them. Besides, the shop was empty. The supervisor was busy and out of our way, so we took the Mickey out of her. It was great fun. We decided that we would stay younger than our years, or we might end up like her.

'Beat you to the café,' Abbey shouted as she started to run.

'That's cheating. You had a head start.'

We were lucky we didn't crash into someone as we came to a sliding halt in the café, laughing and trying to breathe at the same time. We only had a drink. Even the lady serving us was in shock, 'you two not eating? We will have blizzards.' She had laughed.

We were silly all day and doing things that we knew we really shouldn't. We swapped all the cheeses and hams and things about on the pizza counter, and then stood laughing when the others put all the wrong things on the pizzas. We even mixed up our own recipe for the chicken sauce and called it a new "Abbieali" sauce. Some people even brought it. Don't worry, it wasn't anything very bad. Just a mixture of all sorts.

Abbey raced me to lunch where we had cod and chips and a fizzy drink. The lady said something about us eating our lunch and something about that's the girls she knows. We just giggled and sat down asking each other what on earth she was on about. The dinner was lovely, but about half an hour after lunch I was so sick that I was sent home.

'What you doing here? You've not been sacked, have you?' Martin looked amazed.

'No, not sacked, but sick. I feel better now, though.'

'Maybe it was something you ate. What have you had today, or more to it, what haven't you had today?'

'Well, I met Abbey for tea and toast this morning, and I was fine.' I told him about being told off. He just rolled his eyes at me. 'I didn't have anything at break time.' This time his mouth fell open. 'The cod and chips seemed to be fine, maybe it was the mini–iced-ring-doughnut race we had. That might have made me sick.'

'What do you mean "doughnut race", exactly?'

'We were seeing who could eat the most doughnuts in 3 minutes. They were only little ones.'

'No wonder you were sick. How many did you eat?'

'I don't know... about seven... Abbey ate more, but she wasn't sick.'

'I wonder sometimes just how old you two are.'

'That's what our supervisor said, but then, she is a grumpy old cow.' I smiled.

'I've got a flight to France with Kerry and Simon tomorrow night. Is that OK?' He was hesitant to tell me. I couldn't blame him after yesterday.

'That's fine. When will you be back?'

'Saturday night, not late. I'm sorry that I left you out yesterday when we were looking at houses; we just got carried away.'

'That's OK, but you do it again and you will be carried away... in your box. Do you want a cup of tea?'

Martin told Kerry about the trip and nearly caused a riot. 'That's not fair. Why can't we go? What are we going to do?' Sandra and Daisy were going on and on.

'You two are going to stay with auntie Pat. I know you won't mind. She always spoils you. Anyway, I have to work until nine tomorrow night.' I smiled at the thought of all the bed to myself and all the yummy things I could have for dinner.

We had veg lasagne. It was OK, but you get indigestion when the kids don't stop moaning about it.

I was early. I didn't have to get up so early. I don't start work until half past twelve. I think it was the hunger pains stabbing at me that woke me. I told myself to just have toast with a bit of jam. It's hard to enjoy toast and jam when you have visions of a good fry up in your head.

'You're not hungry? I bet it's because you're going to miss me tonight.' Martin hugged me.

'No, I'm starving, but I'm getting bigger by the day. Soon my uniform won't fit me. Anyway, who says I'm going to miss you? I will have all the bed to myself.

'Oh, thanks a lot. I feel very loved.' He grinned.

Kerry was up next and doing my head in. She was so excited today was her last day at school, and she wanted to be early so that she could get everyone to sign her book. All the years I have bellowed and shouted at her to be ready on time for school, and her last day she is up and ready. It drives me mad.

By about eleven o'clock Kerry was home again. They had been allowed to go early. I was so hungry I could have eaten anything, but I couldn't eat a thing as Martin and Kerry were there. So I had to wait.

Everyone was busy, so I took myself off upstairs and got ready for work.

'You're ready early. Don't you like being with us?' Martin laughed.

'I'm in the way here, so I might just as well go off now, and being Friday the traffic might be bad.'

'OK, see you tomorrow. Have a good evening without us.'

'I intend to take care, and Kerry, behave yourself and don't let your dad go mad with the houses.' I gave them a kiss goodbye and left.

The traffic was surprisingly good, and I got to McDonald's in no time. I checked the place out first. I wanted to make sure that there was no one there that I knew. When I felt sure it was safe, I went and ordered a chicken burger and chips. Then I sat in a nice quiet corner. This is how my Fridays should be. I took a lovely big bite of burger to make sure it was real. The supermarket was only next-door, so I could take my time. It was heaven.

As I was changing into my uniform and singing to myself, my supervisor (the grumpy one) came in.

'What are you doing here? You were sent home with a tummy bug yesterday.' She was grumpy.

'I know, but I'm fine now, and I didn't say I had a tummy bug,' I was as polite as I could be.

'Well, whatever was wrong with you, you still should not be here. The company policy says you are not to return for at least twenty-four hours after being sick. What else makes you sick suddenly if not a tummy bug? At your age, you couldn't possibly be pregnant.' She slammed the door after her.

'Now why are you home early? Not been misbehaving again?'

'No, the old bag said I was not allowed back to work for at least twenty-four hours after being sick. I didn't know the company rules. She stuffed a rules book in my hand.'

'Kerry was just doing some sandwiches before we go. Do you want some?'

'Err... no thanks. I'm not hungry.'

'You are being good. All you have had is toast. Are you sure your tummy is OK?'

'Very funny. I'm just trying hard.'

I kept out of the way while they sorted themselves out. They seemed to have a lot of stuff. Don't know how they will be able to lug that around.

It was five o'clock, and I was waving them off. I could have called Pat to tell her that I was at home, but I didn't. She loves having the girls. Her children are older and hardly ever in, so she loves to spoil mine, and the kids love it too.

All alone for the night, I went through the TV paper and sorted my viewing. All the rubbish that Martin won't let us watch will be on tonight. Now what to eat for dinner? Did I want to cook or not? It would be cheaper, so I should really cook. Maybe I should just pick at things and see what I can bung in the microwave... yes, that's it... that's what I will do... Oh, this is going to be a great evening. Now lets see what we have in the cupboards first.

Before I knew it the clock said eleven o'clock, and my viewing plans were coming to an end. I had finished a bottle of wine and various plates of food. The remains of the chicken curry that I had was a small curry I had made and frozen a couple of weeks ago. The half-eaten pork pie crust and pickle was looking pale and dry. The large, now empty, packet of cheese and onion crisps was giving the room a slight pong, and as for the garlic bread... well, what can I say about that? Apart from being sure that I will taste it again at about three o'clock in the morning. Now with slightly wobbly legs, I was in search for something sweet... well, chocolate to be exact.

I plonked the plates and things to be washed in the sink, and then opened another bottle of wine (not really a good idea). I also had some chocolates that I brought earlier. Seeing as I was to be alone, I knew I would like a treat. The wine was probably the wrong decision to make, but for now I was happy. How I wasn't sick after all that mixture, I don't know.

Lizzie (my nice supervisor) was very understanding when I phoned in sick that morning. She said that she had been told I had been sent home sick on Thursday. I felt awful, not just because of the hangover, but because I was not really ill. It was all my own fault.

I was feeling better by the time Pat dropped the girls off. While we had coffee, I asked Pat about changing our gym night. She said it would do me good. That would have been very kind of her if it hadn't been for the way she looked at me when she said it.

Not long after Pat went, the others came home. I could hear Martin saying, 'don't worry, I will talk to her. I'm sure she will be fine.' To this, Kerry said, ' And if she's not, she will more than likely kill you.' They came into the front room, and I pretended that I hadn't heard them come in.

'Hi, did you have a nice time? Did you see the house you all liked?' I smiled, worried about what Martin was going to talk to me about; I had a feeling I would need chocolate.

'We saw loads of houses. The estate agent had got a lot of houses for us to look at together. She was very good and helpful.' Kerry was almost singing.

'The house we liked was sold, but we saw this one... ' He was sounding desperate again.

'It's in the middle of a village?' I snapped. I could feel my hangover coming back.

'It's a small, quiet village.'

'We agreed to go to the country, not a village. There will be people everywhere that I will not be able to talk to.'

'But it will be better for the children to mix with French children. It will help them learn. We can have lessons. The lady said that there are people in France who do lessons... ' He was almost begging... why?

'I will think about it.'

'Well, you better think quickly. We only have seven days. I signed the papers for it, and we get seven days to change our minds.' He was looking at the floor so he couldn't see my face turn a brilliant red colour.

'You did what? Without me, without asking me if I would like to live there? What gives you the right to do that? And what about this place? It's not even been valued yet. I just don't believe you sometimes, Martin. I really don't.' I was yelling so hard I hurt my throat.

'I told you she will go mad. It's going to take mum more than seven days to cool off.' Kerry said calmly.

I plonked myself on the garden bench and cried. I think I cried more out of anger then anything else. I felt my life was being taken over and that everyone had made up their minds and mine for me. I didn't really know what to think or how exactly I felt.

The information on the house was in English. It was a lovely house with out buildings and a nice amount of land. I could hear Martin and Kerry telling the others about the house. They were all so exited. Was I being silly or just selfish? I just didn't know what to do or where to turn. I felt lost and alone.

Martin handed me a cup of tea as he sat down next to me. 'I'm sorry, I should never have signed for the house without talking to you first.'

'You're bloody right there.'

'I just got carried away. There were other people interested in it. It is such a nice house. I didn't want to let it go. I will call the estate agent on Monday and tell her I made a mistake.'

'No, don't do that. You all like the house, and it's a good price. It looks very nice, and I don't really have a choice. So you better call the estate agent, and get this place sold. This does not mean that you are off the hook. You will pay for this dearly, especially if I get there and hate it.' He knew I meant it.

Chapter Eleven

Sunday and I was up early cleaning like a mad thing. The estate agent is coming tomorrow, and I want the place looking like a new pin. The kids are on half term so they have been warned that anyone makes a mess, and you will be sorry.

I was desperate for chocolate, and seeing as I had an upset tummy yesterday I was unable to go shopping. As I cleaned, I searched everywhere for chocolate. I thought that maybe the kids would have some in their room. Maybe a leftover bit of Easter egg that they had forgotten about, but no luck. So I kept cleaning and searching, the more I looked and did not found anything, the more desperate I became. I pulled everything out of the cupboards in the kitchen and there at the back of the cupboard was an out-of-date Snicker. It was not out of date by much, just a month or so, but I didn't care. I did check it over to make sure there were no white bits or furry bits or anything moving. It was fine. I wanted to eat it slowly, but by then I was so desperate that I stuffed half in at once. It was heaven like, more effective than a box of antidepressants. I wish I had found two.

Martin and I went to the shop for a few things, mainly chocolate for me, but I really can't tell you what else we got. It was not as important to me as the chocolate. The rest of the day went by in a kind of haze. I did what was needed. The kids did their own thing and Martin continuously asked if I was OK. I found myself sitting in the front room looking at all the hard work we had put into the place. We have been here seven years and it has taken six and a half of them to get the place as we wanted it, and now we are going to sell it. Suddenly I realized that the bag of mini Mars was empty. I had eaten them all, so now I was angry with myself for eating them. By nine o'clock I had put myself to bed. I just wanted this weekend to end.

Monday and I don't start work until two, so at least I will be here when the estate agent comes at ten, if he is on time.

Maybe I should have a light breakfast like toast or corn flakes, but they might be too messy. I don't want anything that will make a mess. I could skip breakfast, but you always hear how bad it is for you not to have breakfast, so I best have something.

I felt nervous about the estate agent coming. What if our house was not worth much? Then we might not be able to go to France. I began to feel hopeful. My spirits were rising; I treated myself to a king-size Mars. No mess to clean up, besides any excuse for chocolate is better than no excuse at all, is what I say.

To my amazement he was on time and told us that our house was worth more than I ever imagined and that we would have no problem selling it. My hopes were dashed. Martin was beaming and so was the estate agent, but then he was thinking of the amount he will get for selling it.

'If we get the asking price we will be able to pay our mortgage up, and buy the French house outright.' Martin was so excited.

'I'm off to work.'

'It's a bit early.'

'I know, but I have missed a few days and a lot can change in a few days.'

I sat in the café to work with a large coffee (no food) wondering why I was not as excited as the others.

'Hi, what's wrong?'

'Oh, hi Abbey, the estate agent came round today and the house is worth more than I thought.'

'Well, that's good, isn't it?' She looked puzzled.

'Yes and no, we can pay our mortgage and buy the French house outright, but it means we will be going, it just don't feel right.'

'Alice, tell me really why you don't want to go.'

'I don't know, what if I can't learn the language? What if everyone else in the village goes to work? I will see no one. I will be so alone. I will go mad.'

'Well, why don't you do something?'

'Like what? I will have a house in a little village full of people that I can't understand.'

'You're so negative. You're so full of what ifs. You have out buildings. What if you open a café or something? You will get to know people, and it will keep you busy.'

'Abbey, you're brilliant. I will see what Martin says, it will be something new and we could do it together.' At last I could see something positive about going.

Martin couldn't believe the change in me when I got home at about 10.15 p.m. that night. I told him everything that Abbey had said was all for it and said that as soon as we were sold up and got our house in France he would sort out what we needed to do to open it.

'Talking of Abbey, I thought you two were going to the slimming club tonight.'

'No, point me going now. Anyway, we couldn't get our shifts changed so we have to work Monday evenings.'

The rest of the week went in a flash. By Wednesday the house was up for sale. The sign was up, and people were asking why we were moving when told them they said you must come round for a goodbye drink, by the time the seventh person had said that I was beginning to think they were just trying to make sure we go.

By the time Saturday night had come. We had had two couples to view the house, and they both liked it. I was on the early shift, so I was just home in time to see the last couple leave. Martin was sure that they would buy the house.

I had found my reason for moving, thanks to Abbey, and I had lost my appetite, thanks to the excitement. At last I was loosing weight again.

We had just sat down to our shepherd's pie when the phone rang. It was the estate agent. He had had a call on his mobile from the second couple that had taken a look at the house, and they wanted to make an offer. He had told them that someone else was interested so they offered the full asking price. We accepted there and then.

I couldn't believe how quickly the house had sold. Now all we had to do was go to France to sort the house out there.

Sunday morning and Martin was clearing out the garage. You forget how much stuff you have until you move. I helped Martin, and the kids went to Pat's for the day. It took us all day to do the garage, but we sorted a lot of stuff out and went to the dump I don't know how many times. By the evening we were very tired and everything hurt.

Monday and Martin was on the phone with the French estate agent. She said she would send us everything we needed, so that we didn't have to take a trip over. I was hoping we would go over. I would have liked to see my new home, but we did have a lot to do here. I left for work as Martin was emptying out the loft. I was glad to get away. We had been so busy that we had not really eaten all weekend. The weight was just falling off me now. It was great, and I was feeling better in myself. So I promised myself to keep it up and try harder.

Work was not busy. So Abbey and I had lots of chance to talk about the move and the café. She was going on about a leaving party.

'The girls were on about a leaving party, but I don't know if we will have time. I will see what I can do.'

'OK, but don't forget my invite.'

'You're the first on my list. Do you think I should do food?'

'It will be a poor show if you don't.'

'OK, what about lunchtime? Should we make a list of what we need?'

We did do some work that morning, but we were more excited about party planning than making pizza. After Abbey had nagged me to death about my salad and not eating enough we got down to party planning. If I did all the things, Abbey suggested I would have to take out a loan.

I got home to find the contents of the loft all over the front room, and the girls going through it. I could tell sorting the loft was going to take a long time as the children and the packing just don't go.

Who Wants to Diet Anyway?

All week my house looked like as if a bomb had hit it. We had thrown a lot of the stuff away, but we still seemed to have so much to pack. And another thing was how were we going to get it all over there? We hadn't thought of that.

We had signed all we needed to for the French house, and ours was going nicely.. It was easier as the young couple were first-time buyers.

We had just three months to be packed and gone. It sounds a long time, but when your working, dieting and packing up your whole home to move to another country, then three months is not long. Oh yes... and a party to sort out. I might have to skip the party. I will ask Martin about me finishing work about a month before we go.

By Sunday I had got the courage to weigh myself. I had lost a huge 9 kilograms in two weeks. I was so pleased that I decided to treat myself with a chocolate bar or two.

At last we had a moving date, and we had dropped the idea of a party out of lack of time and money. It was going to cost a fair bit to hire a van and take three trips to France with all our stuff. The people who we are buying the house from have said that we can put our stuff in one of the out buildings.

'Martin I don't know how, but I've lost 12 kilograms.'

'That's great, love. Can you help me with this box?'

'Glad he was interested. Just coming,' I told the kettle.

One very busy Thursday evening, the people from three doors down came to ask if we would like to go to dinner with them on Saturday to say goodbye. The children often played together, so we accepted. I wrote it on the calendar so as not to forget we were looking forward to it.

Saturday at work, and Abbey was still going on about how little I'm eating and how pale I looked. I just took no notice but threw a pizza base at her. So we were still as mad as ever. After lunch Abbey gave me an invitation to a party with three weeks time. She said it was a birthday party for her sister, and she had said that Abbey could invite us. I accepted and when I got home, I wrote it on the calendar. I was not the only one writing on the calendar. Martin had been as well. I noticed a lot of evening out on the calendar. We haven't had a social life like this for years. We will have to move more often.

We went to our neighbour's that evening, and Denise had done enough food to feed an army. She had laid out plates with cocktail sausages and cheese on little bits of toast, bowls of crisps and all sorts of things they were to nibble on as we drank. God knows how much she has done for dinner.

Denise was a little plump lady and very friendly, an easy person to get on with. So eating and drinking with her came easy. She was telling me about the special dinner she had prepared and how long it had taken her. She was not moaning because she loved to do this sort of thing for people. 'I can't tell her I'm trying to diet. She will be heartbroken after all her hard work.' I was thinking to myself. I will just have to eat as much as I can.

'Oh, Denise! My favourite prawn cocktail. Look at the amount you have given me. You are bad. It's not good for my waistline.' I joked hoping she would take the hint.

'Waistline! Alice, you are funny. I don't remember us having a waistline.' She laughed.

Talk about being brought to earth with a bump. Martin winked at me and smiled. He knew I was trying to get out of having to eat too much.

Denise had made a lovely dinner with loads of cream and chicken with mushrooms and God knows what else. But it was lovely and Moorish. By halfway through, I had had enough wine not to worry about how much I was eating. I made a real pig of myself and enjoyed it.

The very rich chocolate mousse and brandy snaps that we had for pudding was now lying heavily on my chest along with a headache. It was making for a good night's sleep. I was not sure whether to take the headache pills first or the rennies. But it didn't really matter as long as they both worked. I looked at the clock. It was just past two. In about eleven hours' time, we would be joining Joyce and John for Sunday lunch in their garden. Hope it's a nice day and she does a salad, I thought as I dropped off to sleep.

We were all washed and dressed for our lunch out. My headache was gone and I was feeling pleased to be going out again. The girls were loving all the fuss, and today Simon had been invited. So that made Kerry very happy.

Joyce and John lived across the road from us and loved gardening. So today they could show off all their hard work. It was a lovely garden. All the flowerbed weeded and in wonderful colours. We said our hellos and how are you as John poured drinks for us all.

'As it's a lovely day, we decided not to do a roast. I do hope no one minds,' Joyce was saying.

'That's fine, Joyce. It's too hot to be cooking. Maybe we will make salad today.' I was hopeful.

'We decided to do barbecue instead, and a few of the neighbours are popping in to say their goodbyes,' John explained.

'That will be good, do you want a hand with anything, like chopping the salad?' I offered.

'Salad. Alice, my dear, we are not rabbits. We are having beef and chicken with potatoes and things like that.'

'Sorry, Joyce. I was just trying to help.' I felt a bit disappointed. I really fancied a salad.

Joyce and John were in their early sixties and every bit meat eaters.

'No need to be sorry. Here, let me give you a proper glassful. John is so mean when he fills glasses. He only gives half a glass. I know that's what you should have, but we are friends. Lets have proper glasses.'

We had a great time, far too much to eat again. The cheesecake was repeating on me and as for the punch John made, it was enough to knock your head off.

The next three weeks was nothing but work, packing and dinner parties. I was getting so tired that I told Abbey we could not make it to her sister's party. She was so upset that I had to promise we would be there at half past seven

I was glad I had Saturday off. It meant that we all could lie in bed for as long as we liked. It was past eleven o'clock before we got up. I, for once felt better for getting up so late.

My weight was increasing again and fast because of all the dinner parties that we were going to. I was going to have to sort myself out now that all the dinner parties were almost over. Tonight was the last night out, and I was glad. Not that we had not enjoyed it all, but we were so worn out. We put our best clothes on and headed for the party. As we didn't really know Abbie's sister, we just got her some flowers.

There were a lot of cars in the car park of the hall where the party was organised. The music was already booming outside. So this was going to be one hell of a party.

As we opened the door and went in, everything went quiet and everyone looked at us. I felt a bit panicky. Maybe we were at the wrong party, but that looks a lot like Pat over there. As I looked around, I realised that I knew everyone there. I looked up and saw a huge banner that read, GOODBYE AND GOOD LUCK. Abbey had done a surprise party for us. No wonder she was so upset when I said we couldn't go. I couldn't believe it. She came over to us with tears in her eyes. We thanked her and chatted for a while.

I had said goodbye to all my workmates yesterday when I left work. I had handed my notice in last week so I could be ready to go, but they were all here. Martin's family and mine were there. It turned out that Pat had a lot to do with the party. That's how Abbey knew whom to invite.

Abbey had done more food than we sell in the supermarket, but it was all gone by the end of the evening. The drink flowed freely, which helped with the pain of saying goodbye to each person as they left to go home. We helped to clean up before we headed home with a boot full of farewell gifts.

The last four weeks in England went very quickly. Martin took three trips with Simon to France with all our things. Our home was getting more and more empty. By the last week, all we had was blow-up beds, a cover each and a few things to cook with and my beloved bathroom scales.

This was the hardest week of my life as I said goodbye to my sister and other members of my family whom I was close to. But saying goodbye to Pat was the hardest and to my best friend, who has promised to visit a lot. I know it's not a long way away, but it might just as well be a million miles when you're saying goodbye to people whom you care about and they care about you. We all went to the curry house for our last meal together and retuned to our homes in floods of tears.

Who Wants to Diet Anyway?

We were due to leave England on Monday, the 22 August. On the Sunday, Simon's mother invited us all to dinner. This was lovely as she was a very good cook. Martin, the two girls and me walked home as Simon said goodbye to his mum. I couldn't stay for that as I had said so many goodbyes and cried so many tears. But to see a mother and son saying goodbye, no matter how old he is, would have been just too much for me. But now Simon drives and has a little car. So he can pick his mum up anytime for holidays.

Monday morning and one more long look around the house with tears running down my face.

We had eaten whatever we could find for breakfast. Then we packed the last of our home into Simon's cars and ours. Martin and I put the girls in the car and asked them to stay there. Kerry was going with Simon. So they waited in their car. Martin and I stood in our front room for the last time and thought about the years we had had there just holding each other.

'Come on, love. It's time to go.' Martin pulled me gently.

'OK, I have just one thing to do.' I picked up my scales; put them in the same place I always did and stood on them.

' 85 kilograms. I'm so fat. I'm going to have to go on a diet.'

'Whatever,' Martin grinned as I put my scales on top of the pile in the boot.

Printed in the United Kingdom
by Lightning Source UK Ltd.
135012UK00003B/58-66/P